LETTERS TO C

Words of Healing, Wisdom, and Encouragement

A Compilation Presented By
Jason T. Mahoney

RAIN
PUBLISHING

Raleigh, NC

Rain Publishing
http://rainpublishing.com

Book Cover Design & Layout: John Linzie
Edited by: Dr. Damion O. Lewis
Photography – Nicole D. Campbell

Letters to Our Brothers/ Jason T. Mahoney -- 1st ed.
ISBN 978-1-7328709-5-6

Library of Congress Control Number:2019909102

Dedicated in Loving Memory Of

Rev. TJ Slater Sr.
February 7, 1923 – October 14, 2003

Pastor – Educator – Philanthropist

Rev. Slater made significant impacts in the Public School System,
the AME Church Denomination, and the lives of many individuals
he came in contact with.
Thank you for speaking into our future!

June 1, 2000

Congratulations! Keep on keeping on! I hope you have much success

in the future. Remember, if you can conceive in your heart and be-

lieve it in your mind, you can achieve it.

Much Success,

Reverend T.J. Slater, Sr.

Acknowledgments

My Father, My God, My Lord and Savior, Jesus The Christ
It is with full reverence that I give a heartfelt appreciation to my God for anointing me with the gifts of writing and the performing arts. I shall continue to seek his wisdom and guidance as I continue my life's journey.

My Family & Friends
The love, respect, honor, gratitude, and praise that I have for my loving parents Mr. James E. & Mrs. Katie J. Mahoney cannot be fully expressed by words. I cannot thank them enough for their love, guidance, wisdom, and discipline. I am very thankful to each of you for always standing by my side and supporting my dreams. The sacrifices that you both made for me were not in vain. Thank you for fighting for me when I could not fight for myself. I love each of you abundantly. I cannot thank God enough for his wisdom in granting me the opportunity to have an awesome group of siblings. Being the "Baby Boy" allowed each of you to play a significant role in my growth and development. Thank you for putting up with me throughout these years and being my first role models. I am forever grateful for my loving family members and an amazing group of friends. You have always been there for me throughout this journey. I am honored to have every one of you in my life. I thank you all for your support and prayers.

Co-Authors
To my Brothers that believed in me and the vision of this project, "Thank You!" You answered the call and shared your words of wisdom. I am grateful for your commitment, trust, and support of this project. Our solidarity is an example of our power when we work together in Brotherhood.

Introduction

The nation continues to witness the discrimination, inequality, mistreatment, and marginalization of Black Men. Don Diva Global Magazine (2014) reports, "Society has been discounting the Black Man for hundreds of years." This is proven by the 40-Year Tuskegee Study of Untreated Syphilis in the Negro Male (Brown, 2017), the increased incidents of police brutality of African American Men (Dews, 2018), and mass incarcerations of Black Males (Moore, 2017). Regardless of one's socioeconomic status, age, household composition, career, accomplishments, or skin tone, if he is a Black Man, he at any time can face discrimination, inequality, mistreatment, and marginalization.

What can we do to preserve ourselves? What can we do to support each other? What can we do to protect one another? What can we do to ensure our sons have positive role models? What can we do to be present for our families? In this book, you will find the answers to the aforementioned questions. *Letters to Our Brothers* is a collection of letters, prose, and quotes written by Black Men to encourage, motivate, and support other Black Men. The writings will also challenge Black Men in their thinking, actions, and decisions. The letters will provide Black Men the opportunity to reflect and process their values, dreams, goals, and life in its entirety.

Authors of the letters come from different socioeconomic backgrounds, diverse childhoods, careers, ages, household compositions, religious belief systems, and different life experiences. They were asked to write and express their thoughts in a format that would be both challenging and encouraging. Some of the authors shared their personal stories of overcoming adversity, while others provided tools and techniques for success. Overall, all authors were intentional about ensuring their brothers received a message of hope and love.

You may have received this book from someone who loves you, or maybe it was a book that you decided to read. Regardless of how you encountered *Letters to Our Brothers,* it was placed in your life for a purpose. See, what you hold in your hand is a piece of African American history, an instant collectable item that can be shared with generations to come. No matter the moment in time, this book will serve as a tool to guide you and future generations on their life's journey.

Letters to Our Brothers is also our call to action to ensure that all brothers receive motivation, encouragement, and love from one brother to another. It is our prayer that this book cultivates a deeper sense of self-worth, builds character, and sets a standard of living for every black male, in whose hands it is placed.

CONTENTS

Jason T. Mahoney

RECESS IS OVER 1

James E. Mahoney, Sr.

WHAT YOU NEED IS AVAILABLE TO YOU 9

Dr. Timothy Brown

DESPITE THE CHALLENGES, KEEP A POSITIVE MINDSET 13

Robert L. Mahoney

YOUR DAY, YOUR FAITH, YOUR ATTITUDE 19

Rev. Allen E. Warren

FIND YOUR PLACE IN THIS WORLD 23

Knorphe Byrd, III

BREAK FREE FROM THE LIES.. 25

Dr. Edward E. Bell

WHAT I HAVE, I GIVE TO YOU 29

Rev. Jonathan D. Ford

BUILT ON A LEGACY OF FAITH 31

Marcel Anderson

WHEN LIFE IS TOUGH, DON'T LOSE YOUR MIND 35

Dr. Damion O. Lewis

ADORN YOUR SLEEVE 41

Melvin McLeod

FOR THE JOURNEY TO YOUR DESTINY 47

Evan Augustus

YOUR POWER, YOUR WORTH 51

Darius Warren

HOW TO OVERCOME 53

Cloyed S. Brown, Jr.

BELIEVE AND LIVE 57

David Kornegay

YOUR START DOES NOT DETERMINE YOUR FINISH......... 61

Rev. Devin D. Paylor

DON'T FORGET YOUR CHARGER 67

Derrick Wood

HISTORY MAKERS 73

Edward Teyamo Patten

GET UP 77

Devon Johnson

YOU ARE GREATNESS 79

Charles Ashley, Jr.

INVEST IN THE LIFE YOU DESIRE 81

Dr. Jesse Sanders

EMBRACE YOUR LIFE'S DETOURED ROUTE 83

Roy N. Rasheed

DEAR BROTHERS - MOVE!!! 87

Jonathan A. Talley

WALK THE ROAD 93

Dr. Kenny W. Rose

HELP YOUR BROTHER.. 95

Frederick James

YOUR REAL IMAGE.. 99

Antwaun Arnold

GET FIT.. 105

J. Dwayne Garnett

OUR "SECRET" IDENTITY 107

Dr. Norman L. Collins, Sr.

CHOOSE YOUR ROYALTY 111

Ollie Hooker

YOU CAN 115

Jamar Snow

BUILD WITH HUMILITY 119

Dr. Dwyane N. Elam

DECISIONS, DECISIONS, DECISIONS... 123

Joseph Wrights

A LETTER OF LOVE AND LOSS 129

Rev. Justin M. Barbour

THE VALUE OF BROKEN PIECES 137

Carlton Rowe

WISDOM FOR THE JOURNEY 143

Mark Wood

SURVIVORS.. 145

Hon. Marcus A. Shields

HOW TO GET THERE... 149

Michael Adams

FEARLESS IN PURSUIT OF TRUTH AND LOVE 151

Rev. Jake Sanders, III

COMMAND YOUR C's 155

Michael D. Finkley

DESIGNED FOR A PURPOSE 159

Simeon Hutchinson

ALWAYS BELIEVE IN YOU 163

Troy Hill

CHOICES 165

Brandon S. Douglas

YOUR CHALLENGES ARE BUILDING YOU 167

Wayne Russ, II

WHAT IS YOUR PERSONAL STATEMENT? 169

Keith Jackson

CHANGE YOUR LOCATION 173

IT'S YOUR TURN 175

Meet the Visionary 181

LETTERS TO OUR BROTHERS
Words of Healing, Wisdom, and Encouragement

Jason T. Mahoney, MS, CFWI

RECESS IS OVER

We all have hidden scars from battles we lost.

We all have untold stories that hide our pain.

We all have tears we are ashamed to shed.

We all have hurts that we've had to endure.

We all have been identified as guilty for crimes our hands did not commit.

And we all have experienced marginalization that caused us to question humanity.

But we still persevere.... for we are Black Men!

Dear Brother,

RECESS IS OVER! We no longer have time to play around, hide our talents, stunt our growth, abort our dreams, live in fear, disrespect ourselves, and degrade one another. Our women are hurting, our children are fatherless, our communities are infested with ignorance, and our image as black men is being distorted. My brother, **RECESS IS OVER!** It is time for you to get off the sliding board. Each trip to the top is not worth it when you only find excitement by sliding to the bottom. Please stop swinging back and forth on the monkey bars. There are no accomplishments when you are unstable in your decisions. Stop swinging on the swing set and waiting for

someone to push you higher. For you will never reach your goals by just sitting and depending on someone else to get you there. Get out of the sandbox. There is no need in building a masterpiece on sinking grounds. It is time for you to get off the merry-go-round. You will never get to your destination by going around, and around, and around. Get off the playground! You will never change society, fulfill your true potential, and build future generations when you are always playing around. The bell has rung, and the whistle has blown, playtime is over and now it's time to learn. Class is in session...
RECESS IS OVER!

The first, and most important lesson is "Know Thyself". You will never move to your next level in life without knowing who you are. Therefore, I pose the question, "Who Are You Black Man?" Who are you behind your skin tone? Who are you behind your title? Who are you without your neighborhood? Who are you beyond your body? Who are you without your education? Who are you without the latest fashions? Who are you behind the walls that you've built due to pain and hurt? Who are you behind the smile? Who are you without your partner and children? Who are you without your successes and achievements? Who are you behind the mask? Who are you Black Man? To answer the aforementioned questions, you must first look into the mirror, but not at your reflection, but at the various layers that are covering who you are. How did you get these layers? Did your life experiences force you to wear them? Were they given to you by your parents? What was the pain and hurt that developed your layers? You must allow yourself to be vulnerable and truthful. It is at this point, that you can deal with your layers, develop a plan to address them, and eventually "know the man in the mirror".

My brothers, this is a deeply rooted issue regarding our identity as Black men. For you see, the day our African feet boarded the ship that took us from our homeland, was the day layers were placed upon us to cover our identity. From 1619 to the present day, we have worn many layers that were given to us by society, in addition to those we developed ourselves that caused us to forget who we are. And when we cannot meet the expectations of those self-inflicted or societal defining layers, we begin to display self-loathing and self-sabotaging behaviors. This can be extremely dangerous. For example, when you try to domesticate a wild animal, it will become aggressive because it knows that it's not a house pet. It will do whatever it must do, attack whoever is in its way, and destroy what it must to be free in the wild again. Even if it means risking its own life to the point of death. Truthfully, just as you can't domesticate a wild animal due to this danger, you can't continue to live your life wearing layers that don't define who you are. Therefore, my brother, it is important that you identify the layers, deal with them, and rid yourself of them to know the Black Man in the mirror.

The second lesson is "Innate Worth". Unfortunately, we were never taught this. During slavery, our worth was contingent upon our body structure, our strength, our submission to servitude, how much profit we could bring to our slave owners, and other characteristics that made us a "Good Slave". It is because of this value system that we were sold to the "Highest Bidder". Even after slavery, our worth is still being defined by similar characteristics. Unfortunately, we have placed similar inappropriate value systems on each other as brothers. For example, we may value the behavior of a brother as a "Man" when he has multiple women, while devaluing the work ethic of a brother who follows rules and regulations at work as an "Uncle Tom". Regardless of how we were valued by our slave owners, and how our own brothers devalue us at times, it is important to know that you have "Innate Worth".

"Innate Worth" is your birthright. You were born with it and no one can give it to you or take it away from you. "Innate Worth" means that you are lovable, valuable, worthwhile, acceptable, adequate, good enough, important, and equal regardless if others hate, disrespect, ignore, reject, criticize, judge, and disregard you. Even if you devalue yourself, feel worthless, defective, inferior, unacceptable, or unimportant, you still have "Innate Worth". The things of your past, your present, and your future cannot take away your "Innate Worth". You may have committed some awful things along your life's journey, that caused you to land in prison, loose some things important to you, and be labeled, but you still have "Innate Worth". You may have even seen yourself as a "failure" and be treated as one by your family, friends, and society. But guess what, you are still valuable! "Innate Worth" is not only regarding your actions, but also the actions that have been done to you. There may have been a point in your life when you endured pain, that was caused by someone else, that forced you to question your worth. It may have resulted from termination from a job, rejection by loved ones, your spouse cheating on you, imprisonment, discrimination, childhood abuse, etc. Regardless of their actions to devalue you, you are still valuable, important, adequate, good enough, worthwhile, and equal. When you embrace and understand "Innate Worth", you become more aware of yourself, your self-esteem increases, and you are not easily broken by others' vicious acts towards you. My brother, when you really become aware of your "Innate Worth", you will stop allowing unhealthy people to enter your life, cease negative behaviors, and have a better value system of yourself as a Black Man.

The powerful thing about "Innate Worth" is that once you believe in it, you can withstand life's challenges. You will be able to endure your situations just as situations and not as something that defines your worth. For example, you may not be the most popular guy, the best looking, the class valedictorian, have the best GPA, have the best clothes, be chosen for a job, have a handicap, and even find your name left off the roster. But my brothers, just as NOTHING can separate you from the Love of God, NOTHING that you have done or has been done to you can remove the fact that you are lovable, valuable, worthwhile, acceptable, adequate, good enough, important and equal.

The third lesson is "perseverance". Webster's Dictionary defines "perseverance" as: "persistence in doing something despite difficulty or delay in achieving success." Many times, we have goals and desires we hope to achieve in life. However, the road to getting there may be challenging, painful, and tedious. When this happens, we are quick to throw in the towel and give up, or we may take an easier route that will result in only attaining a portion of our dreams. These methods are called, "Giving-Up or Settling for less". How many times have you had your mind set on something, and because of what it would take to get there, you changed your mind? How many times has someone told you that you can't achieve something, and you decided to stop pursuing the goal? How many times have you "just quit"? How many times have you allowed your past mistakes to cause you to not pursue your dreams? How many times have you just given up because you were not achieving your dreams at the pace you felt you should have? How many times have you failed at the course and you immediately gave up? How many times have you just given up because you did not have the resources and support systems in place to go after your dreams? I can assure you that 100% of all brothers will answer yes to one of the aforementioned questions. This is where perseverance comes in.

For you to achieve your goals, you must utilize some of the characteristics of perseverance. You must be prepared and resilient. Preparation is extremely important in your journey towards your goals. Being prepared simply means having alternate plans at your disposal once you get started. Having additional plans are assets and vital to your success towards your goals. For example, a construction company's buildings will never pass their Fire Inspection if they only have one emergency exit. The company must take the time to carefully map out the additional emergency exits, which may require additional resources. Therefore, when a fire arises, individuals will have multiple escape routes. This simply means that to be prepared, you must invest additional time and energy in assessing and planning for "what challenges and barriers" you may face as you work towards your goals. Once you have identified those items, you will be able to develop a plan of action to address them. This will aid you in addressing items that may hinder your journey.

The concept of resiliency, in correlation to perseverance, means that you will be able to remain productive, as well as withstand and recover quickly from difficult conditions. In simpler terms, being resilient is the ability to "Bounce Back". Resiliency is a concept that is built over time. An example of being resilient is a football team that experiences a major loss during a game but can bounce back and play the next game with enthusiasm. As a black man, our history is built on being resilient. For you see, we transitioned from Kings and Queens to bondage, to emancipation, to segregation, to ongoing discrimination. However, as Black Men, we have always been able to "bounce back" and continue to be inventors, writers, elected officials, doctors, lawyers, teachers, history makers, and the list goes on. Therefore, my brother, you have no excuse not to be resilient! Build your capacity to be resilient by being prepared, open minded, flexible, and by accepting the fact there will be challenges along your journey.

It is my hope that you will apply the aforementioned items within this letter to your life. There is much work to be done for our communities, our families, and generations to come. We no longer have time to play around. Generations are perishing and depending on us to save them. My brothers, with the DNA of your ancestors that is locked down in your bloodline, coupled with the importance of knowing yourself, your "Innate Worth", and the skills to persevere, you my brother have the power to heal our land. However, you must be willing to get off the playground! **RECESS IS OVER!**

Sincerely,
Jason T. Mahoney, MS, CFWI

Jason T. Mahoney is a native of Sumter, SC. He currently holds a Bachelor of Science Degree in Sociology from Francis Marion University and a Master of Science degree in Counseling from Capella University. He has worked in the Health & Human Services Field for more than 15 years. He is a Life Coach, an author, motivational speaker, and Certified Family-Centered Trauma Coach. He is a proud member of Kappa Alpha Psi, Fraternity, Inc.

WHAT YOU NEED IS AVAILABLE TO YOU

Dear My Sons, My Brothers,

I was asked "what are some words of wisdom that I desired to hear from my father, grandfather, or uncles as a child?" I'd never really thought about it. I had never questioned if there was something that I thought was missing from the lessons I learned as a child. I was raised primarily by my mother, who was a single parent of 13 children. I was the second to last. My sisters, being older than me, also helped to steer me in the right direction, as did my community and later, by my stepdad. He took me out, showed me the importance of hard work. He was a great man. Once my sisters married, my brothers-in-law also took me around with them, collaborating on various odd jobs and hanging out.

The thing is, you don't always have to have a "good dad" at home. I didn't have a dad at home in my youth, but I learned that the world was filled with many "father" figures–if you look for them. Search them out, show them respect and they can teach you throughout your life. Connect with good role models and good people. You can take what you learn from them and mold it to fit your life

As young black men give the Lord thanks for what he has done for you. Reassess your life and where you are heading in society. Find out what can be done to make a better future for yourself and for others. No matter where you began, you can do great things, no matter if it's from a single parent home or poverty. Become leaders and overcome the challenges of the world. The very challenges that have too many young folks going to jail are because of ignorance or injustice. You truly are our future. We depend on you as much as you depend on us.

And if you should make a mistake, learn from it. Any of us, at any given time can find ourselves in harmful situations, whether it be through our own fault or not. If you should be one of our brothers who is incarcerated, don't give up, don't give in; even Christ was incarcerated. Do your time and when you get out, step forward and keep your faith, believe in the good Lord, and let him guide you. Put your mistakes in the past and leave them there, everyone can be forgiven. But first, you must forgive yourself. And never look down on a man, unless you are bending to pick him up.

Do not allow people in your life that only take from you and never give. Do not allow people in your life to bully you. Speak up and speak out against it. Remove them from your comfort zone. Do not let what others have done to you send you into shut down. Take control of your destiny, think positively, be focused and go full steam ahead. Life will go on and you must be willing to go on with it. Find someone to talk to that can give you a helpful point of view. We all have been down, but it's up to you to find ways to pick yourself up. Life goes on and you must be willing to go on with it. Don't stay in a situation; you do not have to accept it.

Much Love,
James E. Mahoney, Sr.

James E. Mahoney, Sr. is a native of Sumter, SC. He is currently retired with over 30-years in the carpentry, manufacturing, and landscaping industry. During his tenure with the Georgia Pacific Company, he was elected to serve as the Keynote Speaker for the United Furniture Workers of America and as an advocate for the general laborers. After retirement, he enjoys mentoring, building furniture, and spending time with his family and friends. He is married to the love of his life Katie J. Mahoney. His lives by the motto of "The only time you look down on a man is when you are picking him up".

DESPITE THE CHALLENGES,
KEEP A POSITIVE MINDSET

Dear Brother,

Be encouraged my brother! Life is filled with great opportunities for growth, self-improvement, and amazing rewards. With the right mindset, you can successfully transform a negative situation into a more positive situation. A positive mindset can help you arrive, survive, and thrive during negative times in life. It is important to have a strong belief that you can conquer challenges. There will be times when you may face challenges, setbacks, disappointments, suffer a loss, or have to confront frustrating situations. However, those times are all necessary for growth and self-development. The road to greater success is not always straight, smooth, or easy. If so, everyone would be on the same road. Few choose to take the journey due to the challenges along the way. You may have to endure some bumps, curves, hills, and detours along the journey to greater success, but stay the course. Don't give up.

Sometimes, people give up before reaching their breakthrough, but that doesn't have to be your story. Be sure to keep positive thoughts flowing through your mind, daily. Always strive to remain mentally and physically strong, despite the challenges that you may face. While you are experiencing challenges, don't neglect reading books and exercising your mind and body. You may feel pressured during challenging times. Pressure causes people to adjust their actions and change lifestyle habits. Remember, challenges are designed to help shape you, prepare you, and help make you stronger for future situations. Embrace challenges. Challenges present you with another opportunity to gain strength, knowledge, and help guide you towards becoming the person you were created to be. You were born with a purpose, destined for greatness, and uniquely created in the image of God. You were created to help make an impact with your life and to help make this world a better place by sharing your talents, skills, knowledge, and gifts.

How do you get through challenging times? With a positive mindset and good habits, you will get through the many challenges and come out on the other side as a champion! One good habit that will help you during those times is to consistently feed your mind with positivity. Make a commitment to wake up each day and say something positive about yourself, your current situation, and your future. Strongly believe that your best days are ahead of you and that you have a purpose to fulfill. Believe in your success and your ability to make whatever you want to happen for your life. Work daily to remove all fear and doubt from your mind and replace them with positive thoughts. Let positive words flow from your mouth, no matter what challenges you may be facing. When in a negative situation, we have to quickly transform our mind into a positive state to avoid a mental trap. Over time, you can become mentally exhausted and allow toxic thoughts to flow within your mind if you don't keep your mind renewed. You must consistently remind yourself that: you can do it, you can be better, you will make it, you deserve better, and you will be victorious. It is not enough to only have positive thoughts, but you must also speak it. It is essential to speak it into existence. Speak the following words daily with conviction, "I can do it" and "It is possible!"

Everything that you want to achieve in life demands that you declare it, define it, and devote to it consistently. Declare it by speaking aloud what you want to achieve. Define it by establishing a plan, goals, and a timeline in which you will achieve what you desire. Devote to it by committing to consistent action and seeing it through to completion. Great achievements are possible with a positive mind and constant positive thoughts. You must support your mind by continuously reading good books and guard your thinking. You must be a good steward for yourself and control what you allow to enter your ears, influence your actions, and control your mood on a daily basis. Take charge of your life, be the captain of your day, and be firm with what you believe to be true for you. Your vision is yours and it is ok if others do not believe or understand your vision. Do not waver, do not lower your standards, and do not give up. Keep your head high and keep your eyes on the prize.

Imagine yourself living the best life that you could ever imagine. Imagine yourself standing on the mountain top looking out over your greatest accomplishments because you simply did not give up. Remember that everything that you want and need to get through in life are possible with God, a positive mindset, an attitude of gratitude, and a strong commitment. Beautiful things happen, when you commit to work, to take action daily for growth, refuse to give up, and stay determined to keep moving forward. When you commit to working consistently and taking massive action, you can reap massive results. Your habits impact your future. You must control your daily habits. Be sure to pray, read, and work each day to develop yourself. The difference between you and a person who is living their dreams, is the amount of action that you both take daily. Don't allow excuses and negativity to cloud your vision. Past failures, culture, family, background, or current situations are some of the many excuses that people try to use to justify their reason for giving up. Kick excuses to the curb so that you can live your life to the fullest!

Great transformations happen when we make the decision to take the leap of faith. One main tool that will help you have a successful transformation is to discover your why. Ask yourself a series of questions. Why do you exist? Why do you want greater success?

What do you want for yourself? What do you enjoy? Where do you want to go in life? What makes you happy? Where do you want to see yourself in 1 year, 3 years, and 5 years? You must commit yourself to your why. Your why will drive you. It will keep you going during challenging times. Your why will push you to keep moving forward until something happens. Your why will keep your mentality strong when your body may feel tired. Your why will help you soar to the next level. You know your reason for going through the struggle, for enduring the pain, and for keeping your mind right when everyone else is losing theirs.

What are some key nuggets for greater success? Consistent, positive action is the key to greater success! Great achievements and greater success happen over time when there is consistency in action, good habits, positive mindset, and a strong commitment. You must commit to being happy. Commit to forgiving others and not carrying around dead weight. Commit to being as stress free, as you possibly can. Commit to seeking help and accepting help from others. Commit to cleansing your mind from negative thoughts and negative people. Surround yourself with positive people. Surround yourself with people who are growing and share similar interests. Surround yourself with people who will lift, praise, and encourage you. Establish a support team or join a support group. Get an accountability partner, mentor, or coach, to help guide you through challenging situations. Always remember to pray because prayer changes things, it changes situations and people. Separate yourself from stressful situations. Stop bad habits and replace them with good habits. Stop focusing on negative thoughts. Release doubt and fear from your life. Embrace positivity 100%. Be consistent in developing positive habits and executing positive actions daily. Believe that anything that you want to do is possible. Believe that there is an abundance waiting for you in life. Great opportunities are available in life, but you must own it. You must want those opportunities and you must consistently work to make it happen. Remember that all of your hopes and dreams can become a reality.

The call to action is for you to decide to make a positive change and declare today that you are more than enough. Declare today that you will make it through every challenge, no matter what! Declare today that you will be victorious!

Peace and Love my brother.
Dr. Timothy Brown

Dr. Timothy Brown is a native of Loris, SC. He is a Christian, husband to Dr. Sherita Brown (Insight Family Eye Care), father to two beautiful children (Timothy II & Tycianna), & son to wonderful parents. He is a graduate of Loris High School (2000). He earned his Bachelor of Science in Biology (2004) from Lander University and his Doctorate of Optometry (2010) from the Pennsylvania College of Optometry at Salus University. He is an Optometrist, motivational speaker, entrepreneur, Independent Avon Sales Representative & Team Leader. He enjoys playing tennis, riding bikes with his family, livestreaming with TAB's Multimedia, impacting lives with TAB's Men Ministry, and traveling. One of his daily goals & prayers is to inspire & motivate others! He is a proud member of Omega Psi Phi Fraternity, Inc.

YOUR DAY, YOUR FAITH, YOUR ATTITUDE

Dear Brother,

Today is **YOUR DAY**! It's the day that you honor your past and go after your dreams. You can accomplish anything your heart desires while maintaining a relationship with God, committing positive actions, and having the right attitude.

It is important that you have a relationship with God and always put him first. This requires you to spend time with him in prayer and worship. It is during prayer and worship that he provides you with guidance for your journey. A good way to have this time is to carve out time each day in a quiet place where you can encounter his presence. For me, I often spend time in prayer and worship in an atmosphere filled with nature. It is through the trees, water, wind, dirt, animals, and other natural environments that provides me with an opportunity to experience God in his fullness.

As Black Men, it is important to pay attention to your actions. Many individuals will have preconceived thoughts as to what your actions should be based on the fact that you are a Black Man. Please know that your actions will either make or break you. The easiest action to ensure you are on the right track and destined to have a good day is to wake up with a positive attitude every day. Despite what is going on in your life at this present moment, you have a choice in your attitude. Charles Swindoll stated: *"We cannot change our past...we cannot change the fact that people will act in a certain way. We cannot change the inevitable. The only thing we can do is play on the one string we have, and that is our attitude...I am convinced that life is 10% what happens to me and 90% how I react to it. And so it is with you...we are in charge of our attitudes."* Always remember that you are in control of your attitude and it will dictate the outcome of your day.

It is also important that you maintain a healthy mindset. Often, we find ourselves listening to negative self-talk and other terrible thoughts in our minds. You must have a strong mindset to keep all the negativity out. To exercise and build a strong mindset, practice self-talk. You must also simply cut negative thoughts off whenever you find yourself having them. Immediately shift your mind to focus on positive items, regardless of how small the item is. Overall, a positive mindset will overcome.

It is also important to smile no matter what. Find positive items that make you happy in your own way. Others may think that what makes you happy is "weird". However, do not allow someone else to define your happiness. A great tool to create a smile, is to keep a running list of items that you can do to make you happy. Whenever you find yourself in a sad mood, find something on the list to do.

Most importantly, surround yourself with great family and friends, people that will keep you going. STAY AWAY from negative and unhealthy people. Develop a list of those you spend time with or who are attached to you. Assess the list. Are they adding to the positivity of your life or subtracting from it? This technique will assist you in removing those that are unhealthy for you. Cutting yourself away from them may be hard but holding on to negative people is detrimental to your goals.

The accomplishment of your dreams and a shift in your mindset will not take place overnight. Don't rush it! Use **YOUR DAY** each day and take one step at a time. The end result will be the accomplishments of your goals.

I will look for you at the top of the mountain!

Robert Mahoney

Robert L. Mahoney is a graduate of Clemson University where he received his Bachelor of Science degree in Parks Management and Wildlife & Aquatics Biology. He is currently a SC State Park Manager where he oversees the 7000-acre Cheraw State Park. Robert has received numerous awards and recognition for creating safe places for individuals to have fun, find mental, physical, and spiritual health, and social well-being.

Rev. Allen E. Warren

FIND YOUR PLACE IN THIS WORLD

To all of the brothers who struggle to find their place in this world,

All of us have been granted God-given talents, gifts and graces in order to enhance our lives, and to reach the lives of those with whom we come in contact. It is necessary for each and every one of us to take our rightful place as God has ordained in this world. I know that sometimes the struggles along with the trials are overwhelming, but it is through the struggles and the trials that we are strengthened. We develop character during these struggles. They produce in us perseverance, which in turn builds patience and unlocks the door to our success. I would encourage all of humankind to participate in this thing called life. It is important that you embrace it, love it, and appreciate it. Allow yourself to be used as a major contributor to the ongoing development of yourself and others who find themselves struggling. In times of adversity, you don't just have an obstacle to deal with. No, more importantly you have a choice to make. Your problem introduces you to yourself. No problem will ever leave you the same way it found you. What we believe is what we can achieve. As a man thinks, so he must be. If it is to be, it is up to you to take hold of your life and make your mark. Be what God has called and ordained you to be within this earthly realm. No one can stop you, but you. Rise up, men of valor, your future is waiting. Your dream has a date with destiny.

Your Brother,
Rev. Allen E. Warren

Rev. Allen E. Warren is a native of Alamance County, NC. Rev. Warren served in the United States Navy, Concerned Citizens, Alamance Civic Affairs, is former Vice President of the Ministers Alliance of Alamance County, former Board Member of the Commission of Allied Churches of Alamance; and the Chairman for Community Watch for Alamance County. He received numerous awards as General Manager of Byrd's Distribution Center for 18 years. Rev. Warren is also an Honorary Member of the Burlington Police Department and the Coordinator of the Sons of Allen for the Eastern District. Pastor Warren has extensive pastoral experience, leading over six churches over his 30+ years of ministry. He is married to the love of his life Mrs. Linda Warren and together they have five children and six grandchildren.

BREAK FREE FROM THE LIES

Dear Young King,

You have been lied to your entire life! Everything that has been taught to you, shown to you, and brought into your experience is a deception. These lies have been allowed to invade our being and re-define our limitations for many generations. They have us feeling like helpless victims, overwhelmed with hopelessness when problems arise. Yes. You have been lied to about who you are physically, historically, and spiritually.

The world knows that if they keep repeating these lies, you will remain in a state of turmoil. Without knowledge of self, you will be imprisoned in their strategically designed shackles. They know that by holding on to these lies, you will conform to an ideology of enslavement that so many of our people have already fallen prey to. Let's take this moment to unveil the truth of who you really are. Only through self-discovery will you tackle turmoil, shatter shackles, and conquer conformity.

Physically. Black men today are believed to be born inferior. Throughout your life they tell you that you need medication to learn properly, Special Education to keep up with the majority, and validation to succeed. The truth is that you were the originators of Math, Science, Architecture, Music, and Philanthropy! The melanin that coats your black skin is not unlike the fictional element, "Vibranium", making you dominant over all other men. It is the most valuable substance in the world and studies have shown that it is a superconductor, capable of converting limitless amounts of energy. In ancient times black skin was not seen as a weakness, but as a sign of intelligence, power, and royalty!

Historically. You were told that we came from slaves who were brought here centuries ago. In actuality, our history is much richer than slavery. We are the fathers of civilization and all other men came from us! Historians are now able to prove that our ancestors were traveling the world long before anyone else. Our ancestors were the architects of the great pyramids in Egypt and were the inspiration for all other cultures you see today. We thrived so profoundly in Africa that we shared our knowledge to help civilize Europe and usher them out of the Dark Ages.

Spiritually. Not only were you made in the Creator's image, but the Creator dwells within you. The truth is that you are indeed a Creator! You have the ability to literally **create** and change any aspect of your life. Black men have been proving this for millennia, but the information has been stripped from us. Through the careful focus of your dominant thoughts, emotions, and intentions you can add color to your situation and paint the canvas of your life.

Moment of Truth. You are an infinite being with unlimited potential that can overcome any obstruction. To the man who stands in his truth, problems are seen as opportunities. Opportunities for us to define and declare to the world who we think we are. Just who do you think you are black man? Who do you think you are when facing the opportunity "growing up in poverty"? Who do you think you are when facing the opportunity "chronic illness"? Who do you think you are when experiencing the opportunity "desperation", "broken home", "school", "single parent household"?

You are the progeny of original, physical, historical, and spiritual greatness. The problems (opportunities) that come to you are microscopic next to the unlimited potential that is inside of you. Call on this power every moment of every day by boldly and unapologetically answering the question, "Who do you think you are"?

Sincerely in Truth,
Your Brother Knorphe Byrd, III

Knorphe Byrd, III is a native of Columbia, SC. A software developer native to South Carolina. He has served in leadership, advisor, and mentoring positions with various organizations to uplift the community. While not working he enjoys traveling, being a "Funcle", and volunteering at a correctional facility where he works with soon to be released inmates on building their speaking and communication skills. He is a proud member of Alpha Phi Alpha Fraternity, Inc.

WHAT I HAVE, I GIVE TO YOU

Dear Brother,

I hope things are well with you. I want to share a part of my legacy with you. You mean that much to me. Throughout my life, I have been blessed with so much. Because I have abundance, it is only right that I share with you. You are a part of my living will. After much thought, I am leaving you in my Will. However, what I am giving to you, make sure to use *these things* now:

To you, My Brother:

I give to you *Grit.* In the face of challenges, don't give up; be determined.

I give to you **Understanding.** Never doubt, there are those who don't want your success. You have the ancestral genius to rise (Remember Maya Angelou, "Still I Rise")—understand that you were built to survive!

I give to you **Respect.** Honor yourself by being what others dare to be.

I give to you **Awareness.** Know who you are; never allow anyone to tell you what can't be done—especially if you want to do it.

Finally, I will to you **Responsibility.** Be responsible and diligent in charting your course for success.

Brothers remember James Baldwin! Well, he said: "Our crown has already been bought and paid for. All we have to do is wear it." My Brother, just put on your crown! You are a King!

I have affixed my signature to this letter, attesting to my sincerity and love for you. Be it known, that if I can, you can, too.

Dr. Edward E. Bell

Dr. Edward E. Bell is a native of New Bern, NC. He is a sought-after speaker and community activist. He is a former program administrator for a federally- funded after school program. Dr. Bell is an author and has written peer review articles that addresses the plight of African - American males. Also, his professional experiences include being a parent educator, teacher, social worker, non- profit executive, school counselor, and a college professor. He is a proud member of Alpha Phi Alpha Fraternity, Inc.

BUILT ON A LEGACY OF FAITH

Dear Young Brother,

As you go through this journey of life, there are going to be many challenges and obstacles you must face. Through these challenges, it is important to remember that you were built on a legacy of faith. A Gospel musician, Donald Lawrence, mentions in a song that you come from royalty. You are a part of an aristocratic dynasty. Understand that one of the main goals of the enemy is for you not to figure out who you are and the potential you have in this life. My young brother, you were built on a legacy of faith. I want to share with you the story of a young man named Daniel, and how he discovered the legacy that was within him.

Daniel's Story

As I laid there tossing and turning, all I could hear was that alarm clock going off in my mother's room. Normally she'd call my name loudly, but that morning was so different. I thought to myself, any moment now and she will be screaming at the top of her lungs. She never called my name. I proceeded into her room. I called her name several times, but no response. I began shaking her and calling her name. Still no response. I noticed that her eyes were open, and she was a little cold. Immediately I called 911 and my aunts.

After 911 arrived, they pronounced my mother was dead. All I could think about was, what is going to happen to me now. My mother was my all in all. For you see, I was an only child, my father was never around consistently. In fact, I did not really know my father. Years prior to this, my father and I had to take a blood test to prove he was actually my father. I went to court and watched this man say that I was not his child and my mother was just a woman he felt sorry for and decided to help. So, tell me, what am I to do now?

My mother never spoke negative things about my father to me. I would ask my mother questions about why he would not "claim" me or ever keep his promises to me. Her response was, "It will be okay," and "Not to worry about it." I would express my hate for him, and she would always remind me that if it were not for my father, I would not be here today. I was also reminded that regardless of how I personally feel, I am to always honor my mother and my father.

Well now, my mother is gone, and the question becomes what am I going to do? My father I guess was contacted, but he did not reach out to me. At this time, my heart was so heavy—so many questions going through my mind. Who is going to take care of me now? Just what am I supposed to do? A fourteen-year-old kid left to figure this out all alone. Nobody could understand the pain, the hurt, and the confusion I was feeling. I just needed somebody to hold me, hug me, wipe the tears, and tell me it is going to be alright.

After my mother's funeral, still no father in sight. Not one word from him. The time has come for my family and the courts to decide who was going to finish raising me. As I tried to make sense and figure out the next move for me, I heard a voice instruct me on how to proceed. This voice was very gentle, the voice said, "Daniel you will be alright, for I will take care of you. You got a long road ahead but put your faith in me. If you trust me with just a little, you will see that I will forever have your back. I will provide for you at all times. And

*whenever you need me, I will show up and make everything al-
right."*

*This voice was the voice of God, and He was so right. Months
later, my mother's stepbrother and wife adopted me. My uncle
and aunt I barely knew took on the task of raising me and
providing for me. Years passed, and I eventually grew into
adulthood and God remained true to His promise, especially
through my rough and trying times. There was never a time
that God did not have my back, or he was not willing to fight
my battles. In addition, all it took was a little faith.*

*As for my father, years later I learned the power of for-
giveness. I had to learn that I could not be mad at my father,
simply because he was never taught how to be a father. He did
not know the importance of being in my life. Besides, I never
missed a beat. Anything I ever needed; God always provided.
So, my father and I developed a relationship and we have a
level of respect for each other.*

The story of Daniel is the testimony of my life. I am sure my story may seem sad to many and even familiar to others. I know I am
not the only person that has or will experience the things I mentioned, but the main thing is that we all must remember that faith is
the key to get through anything. It was my faith that allowed me to
come out on top of life's circumstances. I could have been an emotional wreck for a majority of my life, or I could have lost my mind.
But it was all because of my faith that today, I can share my story. It
is my hope to reach out and help my younger brothers who will experience the pain that I endured.

In closing, let me share with you your legacy. In the bible, there
is a story about a man named Job. His story explains God's relationship to human sufferings and invites us to trust God's wisdom and
character. Throughout Job's life, he experienced the death of his
children and loss of all his possessions. He had every reason to lose
his faith in God, but Job held onto his faith and in the end, every-

thing he lost was restored. The bible says Job was blessed with double for his trouble because of him keeping his faith.

My young brother, always remember that we are descendants of many people that had Job's experience. Our ancestors were people of faith, they held onto their faith, and God kept His promises to them. Just as God blessed them, so will he bless us if we continue to stand on our faith. You are built on a legacy of faith. I challenge you to remain faithful to God, no matter what life brings your way. Always remember that even in the storms, you will endure. You are blessed right in the middle of the storms. God will always have your back, if only you just let Him.

Love & Abundance,
Rev. Jonathan D. Ford

Rev. Jonathan D. Ford is a native of Fayetteville, NC. He holds a Bachelor of Arts degree from North Carolina A&T State University, a Master of Public Administration from North Carolina Central University, and a Master of Theological Studies from Liberty University. He is currently employed with University of North Carolina as an Educational Training Specialist. He is the Senior Pastor of St. Paul AME Church in Kenly, NC. A gifted musician, Rev. Ford has worked with several choirs in North Carolina and Louisiana. His passion is to help a church grow by stimulating excitement and enthusiasm through the discovery of the fullness of God's love. He is a proud member of Kappa Alpha Psi Fraternity, Inc.

WHEN LIFE IS TOUGH,
DON'T LOSE YOUR MIND

Dear Young Man,

Do any of you remember the song by DMX called Party Up (Up in Here)? One of the main lines of that song is: "Ya'll gon' make me lose my mind, up in here, up in here." If you don't remember this song, it was released back in the year 2000.

Have you ever been caught off guard in life and didn't know what hit you? Did you ever feel like you would lose your mind after going through some tough times in life? When life is going well for you and all of a sudden you get knocked off your feet, how do you get up from that moment? In 2012, I was caught off guard and knocked off my own two feet. It was the moment when I was captured in a home evasion for 2+ hours and didn't think I would even walk out alive.

The robber held a gun in one hand and a pole in the other. During this home invasion, the robber began to shove me in the bathroom and started to handcuff and blind fold me. He told me that if I did everything he said, I may live. So as time went on, all I could think about was how would I survive this home invasion. I did everything I could to survive in that moment. It was a tough situation, but I held my stance and did everything he told me to do. Even as he began to hit me with the pole and gun throughout the night, all I could do was take it.

How many hits have you taken in this life? Who was your protector during that moment? If you got into a tough situation, who could you call on right now? In that moment, I didn't think it could get any worse, until he began to call me names and tried to damage my identity. How many people have tried to damage your identity by saying nasty things about you that you know were not true? Don't believe them because you have something special to give the world. You see, I didn't think what I went through was real at first, until the robber continued to beat me repeatedly with the pole. I didn't think I was going to make it out alive.

As he pulled down my pants, he began to shove the pole into my anus repeatedly (25+ times). That was the first time. Later, he shoved the pole into my anus again (25+ times) and my mind, my body, and my soul couldn't take anymore. Please don't be shocked by what I just said young man. Sexual assaults happen more often than you think. Research shows that 1 in 6 young men will be sexually assaulted before the age of 18. It's something we don't talk about often, but it happens.

During this situation, my internal being was damaged so badly that it caused me to live with a colostomy bag for 6 months. You see, I went through multiple surgeries that caused me to be hospitalized for 4 weeks without eating any food. It was a true crisis. It was also a tragedy and a disastrous moment for me. I went through psychological and spiritual counseling. So, if you have ever gone through something and didn't get the proper help you needed, please don't be afraid or ashamed to get the help you require. It helps more than you think. Talking to a professional counselor doesn't make you crazy. Just submit to the process and plug into the outlet of wise counsel. It was the counseling that truly helped me gain my confidence back, but the most important part that helped me–was God and prayer. The prayer from my family, friends and strangers.

Think about the things that have caused you to almost lose your mind. Who did you have in your corner? How did you respond to that situation? Psychoanalyst, Erik Erikson says, "how you respond to your situation can dictate or determine your final destination." So, believe in where you're going. Remember that "Greater is ahead of you". Just believe it and you can achieve it. Erikson also said, "that a crisis is not a catastrophe in your life." So, when you deal with a tragedy or disaster in your life, it doesn't have to be the end of the day for you. That moment, and tough experience, can become a turning point in your life. I personally agree with Erikson young man. I also understand that a life crisis can bring you to an unexpected destination (either good or bad). According to Erikson this term, crisis, implies that tension and conflict are necessary to the developmental process and some would argue that point. But in my life experiences, I've grown to believe his words and research to be very true. So, no matter how hard you try to live a good and healthy life, there will be some difficult days ahead of you, and it's so important to learn how to respond to those difficult moments, because we will all experience some type of crisis in our life. However, it's how we respond to those crises that can help push us in the right direction. Keep moving in the "right" direction. So, think about how you respond to your situations next time.

Now, I want you to imagine a car crash that you've seen or been in before. What are some of the most lasting images that come to mind? Is it the broken headlights? Is it the dents and scratches on the car? Or is it the broken window or flattened tires? I'm sure what you see matters, but no matter how damaged the outside of the car may look, you see the most important part in a car crash is the driver. The driver. I said the driver. The person who is driving the car. And that's what we have to focus on when life gets tough and it feels like we will lose our minds after a major accident. We must recognize that our internal parts are just as important. That's where we can truly heal from those tough moments.

When was the last time you ever felt like you were going to lose your mind through a tough situation or circumstance? Have you ever felt like no one would truly understand what you were thinking (for real for real)? Even if they thought they knew what was going on in your mind? If they only knew how your neurotransmitters really worked in your brain. I only say this because no one (human) will fully understand everything that goes on in our minds. Only God himself does. If that is the case, it's important to consult with God when our mind begins to linger from his will in this life. We must continue to understand that the mind is powerful, and it is a terrible thing to waste. I pray that you can keep your mind focused as much as possible on God, even through the good times, so that when something terrible happens in your life, you won't lose your minds up in here, up in here. As you continue to reason and think about the daily events that happen at work/school, in your family, and especially in your own life, keep your mind on the things which are above (heaven) before you lose your mind, "up in here, up in here" like (DMX) said in his song. Just remember, when life is tough, don't lose your mind.

Your brother,
Marcel Anderson
Best Selling Author: Still Living: A Victimized Man's Journey: I'm Purposed to Live

Marcel Anderson is an Author, Speaker, and Urban Soul Contemporary Gospel Artist, whose roots in gospel music began at an early age. A native of Spartanburg, South Carolina Marcel was raised among a powerhouse of musicians and singers, which is where he discovered one of the many passions God had placed in him, which was singing. He is founder and CEO of Accelerating Men Inc., a nonprofit community faith-based organization that mentors young men ages 10-18. His book Still Living – A Victimized Man's Journey, has been listed #2 on Amazon Kindle Download top 100 Best Seller list under Men's Development Growth. He is a proud member of Kappa Alpha Psi Fraternity, Inc.

ADORN YOUR SLEEVE

The Sleeve

Iago: It is as sure as you are Roderigo,

Were I the Moor, I would not be Iago.

In following him, I follow but myself;

Heaven is my judge, not I for love and duty,

But seeming so, for my peculiar end;

For when my outward action doth demonstrate

The native act and figure of my heart

In complement extern, 'tis not long after

But I will wear my heart upon my sleeve

For daws to peck at. I am not what I am.

– Shakespeare, Othello, Act 1, Scene 1, 56–65

My Brothers in Life,

The garments we wear speak volumes. Accordingly, clothing may be considered an essential element in its ability to aid our efforts to describe ourselves to the world around us. It is a simple truth that we are all born naked. But it is by our personal design that we shape and mold the persona we share with others. Interestingly, there are those among us who have a single, specific persona that is not only unique to them, it is embodies who they really are–no additives, no artificial ingredients, no false representation. Like a high-quality cut of steak, it encapsulates the senses of those who are able to enjoy it; to savor it.

That steak of course is taken from a cow that has been groomed for that purpose. By that I am saying that yes, it was bred for the slaughter. However, to ensure it is tender, to maintain its indistinguishable flavor, the processes that ensured the cow's breeding, birth, grooming, nurturing, and eventual slaughter, were done in a manner to make certain that the final consumer would dine on an exquisite meal. A meal whereby there would be no question as to the quality of the meat they were partaking. In this sense, the steak's persona would hold true. With that being addressed, it is not only desired but necessary that all men take note of the persona they share with the world; the image they present. Would you say your persona is clearly exemplified in all that you do or say? Would you liken yourself to fine cut of quality meat? Of course, not for the slaughter, but could you agree that who you are, is who you share with the world? Or perhaps your personas are many.

It can be inferred that a single persona is beyond the reach of some individuals. So much so that we might be inclined to say that depending on the situation, the circumstances, setting, or the parties involved, our persona shifts to match. We become chameleons. Chameleons are a scientific wonder–or so I reasoned as a child. It can be considered fanciful how they convey to the world who they are and perhaps, how they are feeling. The key here is that their bodies are designed to allow them to convey that persona; to emote. Would it be nice if we could all say the same? To say that we emote.

For men our personas, whether they be one or many, are evident of who it is that we wish to share with the world. However, unlike the quality steak that can't be imitated or the chameleon whose abilities to self-emote, we are trained to project personas deeply rooted in hyper stylized images of masculinity. Men are strong. Men alone, or so we are taught, bear the weight of the world on their shoulders. All men must be capable leaders who chart their own paths and ensure the success of those under their care (e.g. family, spouse, children). To do such things, men are conditioned to emote traits that may be more likened to a stone. In other words, we must be strong and hard, rigid and unmoving, indominatable, and unfeeling. Unfeeling may seem unsettling in this description, yet men are taught to practice the skill of withholding emotion for fear of moving from the hard stone to something less rigid–something soft.

We do ourselves a disservice by not sharing with the world who we are. We rob them of the ability to get to know the truth of who we are behind the hyper stylized personas derived from archaic beliefs about who and what a man is. Unfortunately, the world is just a bit dimmer due to the purposeful shading of your distinctive, luminescent light. However, all is not lost. There is still time to reclaim your hidden light and allow all to be cast within its glow.

To begin, you must reflect and acknowledge the truth of who you are beneath your current visage. Next consider what is special, profound, and God-given within you that must be delivered unto the world in which you have been cast. Sounds easy doesn't it? Be careful. Project not what you have been taught to share. Hide not what you have inside. Make the conscious decision to accept, for yourself, all that you are, even the parts of yourself that you despise. Because they too are a part of you. You gain power by shaping your image with the elements that have been crafted for you. Alas, you will reclaim your ability to align your spiritual interior with your mortal exterior. Learn to wear your emotions on your sleeve.

Men may find themselves rebuked for indulging their flowing emotions and allowing them to seep through the very surface of their being. Like sponges, we attempt to absorb the moisture of emotions dripping within the core of our being. We fear to be described in opposition to the image of man. The image recounted earlier that is hard, cold, and strong. In doing so, we create the perfect paradox. We fear ridicule of being falsely identified, while we falsely exemplify the person we think the world wants us to be. This may be inextricably linked to the internal processes of bondage that we subject ourselves to. It can be witnessed in the masculine refrain from shedding a tear when we are happy. Observed in the subjugation of affection for our loved ones. Expressed by our disdain for any signs that might cause questions to arise regarding our masculinity juxtapose traits we align with femininity. We have placed ourselves in slavery and unknowingly become our own oppressive masters. Thus, we cannot be who we were destined to be.

My charge to you: Adorn your sleeve. All that is within you. All that you are feeling and desiring must be set free. It must be acknowledged–give it a name. Allow it to decorate you as a soldier decorates his uniform with the medals and badges that immediately tell the world who they are and what they have done. Bely not your strength in reclaiming who you are and what you were meant to be; what you were put on this earth for. There was a reason you were brought here. Here, meaning: in this moment, in your space, in your setting, in your circumstance. There was some profound reason because you were made in His image, and that alone charges you with the responsibility of conveying that to the world. Honor the process called life that has been afforded to you to craft you into what you were destined to be. Own it. Adorn your sleeve, wear your heart upon it. And let all in your presence know that you are who you are; no falsities or pretense. Announce that you my friend, are here.

Your Brother,
Dr. Damion O. Lewis

Dr. Damion Lewis is a graduate of Elizabeth City State University, East Carolina University, and Liberty University. He has served as an educator for 15 years. As a former English Literature teacher, he professes a personal passion and interest for the written word. He is currently a Teacher Trainer-Professional Learning Specialist for Wake County Public School System.

FOR THE JOURNEY
TO YOUR DESTINY

Dear Brother,

I write this letter in honor of your destiny. I believe in your dreams, your goals, and your heart's desires. You have what it takes to get you there, but you must believe in yourself. Know that the journey will not be easy, but what God has put inside of you will help you to endure. As you journey towards your destiny, remember the importance of God, Family, and Education.

Always be steadfast in your relationship with God. In life, you will be exposed to many people, places, and things. The exposure may often challenge your beliefs in God and cause you to question the essence of his existence. Please know this as a trick of the enemy. To be prepared for these situations, stay in your word, stay prayed up, and surround yourself with true believers. There will also be some hard, cold, and lonely days throughout your journey. However, as long as you remain in God's word, his Grace and Mercy will always follow you.

I also encourage you to realize the importance of family. Love them. Celebrate with them. Be there for them. Your family is who you are, and you exist because of them. Sometimes you may find some challenging and tedious moments in life, but you can always come home to family. Your family will provide you the healing, love, and restoration that you need to continue your journey. If you do not have a positive relationship with your family, this is an opportunity for you to create your own with close friends. The bottom line is, it is important for you to have healthy relationships with others. We are humans and cannot live in this world alone.

It is also important for you to embrace education. I started to embrace education at a late stage in my life. However, once I realized its power, I am always going after it. Educating my mind has become a part of my daily living. Any teachable moment is educating the mind. It is important to note that education goes beyond the classroom. It may be learning how to operate heavy machinery or listening to words of wisdom from an elder. Education gives us the knowledge we need to pursue our dreams. It teaches us about the world around us and allows us to build our own thoughts and opinions. It will give you the tools needed to matriculate through life, engage in social circles, and allows your voice to be heard. In other words, education is like oxygen, we need it to live in the world. If you have not embraced education, I need you to start today. Once you become educated, it is yours. No one can take it away from you! It is the gas that will fuel your destiny. An educated black man is a force to be reckoned with.

My brother, it is my hope and prayer that you will be steadfast in your relationship with God, embrace your family and friends, and invest in your education. These lessons have truly helped me on my journey, and they will help you as well. However, you must commit yourself to the process and never allow anything to turn you around. I believe in you!

Your Brother,
Melvin McLeod

Melvin McLeod is a native of Sumter, SC. He is a Senior Corporal with the Sumter County Sheriff's Office. He has worked in law enforcement for more than 15 years. He has developed and hosted community sports clinics to provide youth with an opportunity to receive mentoring, engage in character building activities, and practice communication skills. He enjoys working with the youth and seeing them achieve their goals. He is married to his high school sweetheart, Hester McLeod. Together they have two children.

YOUR POWER, YOUR WORTH

Dear Young Black Men,

Do you know your worth? Do you know how much you can do for the world? Success is not just what you accomplish in your life, it is about what you inspire others to do. You have great power within yourself. Take in everything that you learn, whether you learn it in school formally or informally from a stranger. Also, rely on God to mold and mature you. Realize that everything will not go your way at all times, and that you can't control every situation. Having peace is better than being right. Starting off on the wrong foot doesn't always mean things will end badly. You have the power to change yourself, which will affect your situation and those around you. Take the responsibility to make your mark, somewhere, positively.

I'm rooting for you.

Sincerely,
Evan Augustus

Evan Augustus is a native of Newport News, VA. He currently holds an associate degree in Information Technology from Community College. He is currently employed with The City of Newport News as a 911 Senior Telecommunicator. He is also a Licensed Ordained Minister. His greatest accomplishment is having the opportunity to give assistance to someone in need. I hope my contribution gives someone a little light in a dark world.

HOW TO OVERCOME

Dear Brother,

It is with a grateful heart and a humble spirit that I pen this letter to you. It is my hope that you are encouraged, and your faith is renewed. Within this letter you will find portions of my testimony, the keys to overcoming adversity, and a prayer of endurance.

In life we are often faced with many challenges. Some of these challenges can cause us to question the essence of our existence. We may begin to question God and decrease our desire to live. Well, at the age of 6, I found myself in that state of mind. When all my friends were enjoying their childhood and living carefree, I found myself facing death, grieving over the loss of a close friend, and posing the question: "Why Me?" I was on the schedule to die, but God had appointed me to live. For this reason, I am able to write these words to you.

When I overcame death as a child, I was ready to live my adult life. However, as I grew, so did my life's challenges. I was placed on dialysis, informed I needed a kidney, faced multiple hospitalizations, and endured a period of blindness. Being blind was one of the biggest challenges I had to endure. I was ready to give up and throw in the towel. I felt that God had forsaken me, but it was when I could not see that I saw the most. In my blindness, I realized the importance of staying in the Word of God, maintaining a relationship with my family and my support system, having hope, and making the decision to fight.

Although I could not see the words within the Bible, I asked my mother to read to me. I even would "talk" to Siri and ask her to speak Bible verses to me. The Word encouraged me, motivated me, and gave me the strength to keep going. It was through the word that I remained steadfast in my fight to live. Not only did the word help me on my journey, it also helped bring me closer to my family and friends. Regardless of how challenging things became, they always spoke life into me and over me. When I had given up the fight to live, they fought for me to live. They prayed with me, stood by me, poured into me, and helped me. With them by my side, I was kept in perfect peace.

As mentioned before, it was in my blindness that I was able to see. I can recall one day opening my eyes in hopes to see, but all I could see was darkness. No matter how hard I tried to focus, darkness was all that I could see. But I still believed and made the decision to continue fighting. Eventually, my sight was restored.

My story may appear to be one that would cause other individuals to give up, but when God is on your side you can never give up. I would not have been able to make it without:

1. Reading, studying, and applying the Word of God to my life.
2. Maintaining a good relationship with my family.
3. Surrounding myself with individuals that prayed for me and with me.
4. Always having hope.
5. Continuing to fight and never giving up.

If you apply these 5 items to your life, you will be able to overcome any challenge that you may face in life.

You may be going through some things in your life but if you keep the course, things will work out. My mother always said, life's situations are like seasons, you must be prepared for the weather the season may bring. Just like I wear my warm jacket to stay warm from the winter cold, in my seasons of challenges, I put on the armor of God to withstand the situations that come with the challenge.

My dear brother, I pray that my testimony has renewed your faith in God. I send God's covering over your life. I send you hope for a great tomorrow. I send you the will to fight when life's storms are raging. And most of all, remember it is in your challenging moments, when you will find the answers to your destiny. Remember, it was when I could not see that I saw the most.

Be Encouraged,
Darius Warren

P.S.

When this letter was initially written on April 7, 2019, I was on the waiting list for a pancreas and kidney. However, on May 1, 2019, God answered my prayers, my family's prayers, and the prayers across the world by granting me a new pancreas and kidney. Always remember, "What God has done for others, he will do the same for you." Keep the faith!

Darius Warren is a native of Mebane, NC. He has worked as a Dietary Aide, Sound Engineer for various churches, and Community Volunteer. Darius is a passionate individual that loves God and loves to serve his fellowmen. He enjoys mentoring, volunteering, and inspiring others. He has volunteered with Orange County Parks and Recreation mentoring and empowering youth. He often uses his personal testimony to help others realize God's power in their life.

BELIEVE AND LIVE

John 5:6-9

When Jesus saw him lying there and learned that he had been in this condition for a long time, he asked him, "Do you want to get well?" "Sir," the invalid replied, "I have no one to help me into the pool when the water is stirred. While I am trying to get in, someone else goes down ahead of me." Then Jesus said to him, "Get up! Pick up your mat and walk." At once the man was cured; he picked up his mat and walked.

Dear Brother,

Beloved, if I could focus our attention to one portion of the scripture: "he asked him, 'Do you want to get well?'" Beloved, I know you may not be a big bible reader, but the HOLY SPIRIT brought me here and I must be obedient. Beloved, the focus of this letter is that of faith and how it impacts your daily life. Beloved, I come to you from a standpoint where I understand that things have been hard in our country. I speak from a from a stance acknowledging a lack of employment opportunities. I address you from a perspective that affirms skyrocketing debt levels. I am coming from a vantage point wherein I have observed the steady rise in death rates. They too seem to be at an all-time high, where senseless crimes seem to be the norm for today's society. Although I come from a place of under-standing, I ask this question to each one of you: Do you believe that GOD can take care of your situation? I ask this because that is what CHRIST was asking this man who had been lame his entire life. The question of whether you believe that GOD can heal you? So, my question will be the same. I know that sometimes life can get you down. I know that for most of you, like Langston Hughes, life for you hasn't been "no crystal stair". I know that life has been rugged and hard, but my question for you, is do you believe? Will you be-lieve? While I was at church today, the word my pastor brought from GOD was live. And that is what GOD has for each one of you, live. Beloved, I know that this is hard for you to believe. But everything is going to be okay. All you need to do is believe. I know the devil has told you that it wouldn't be okay, but the devil is a liar, because GOD said you will live and not die. Sometimes we have to praise GOD that the devil is a liar. Why, because the devil told you that your family was going to fall apart, but GOD said not so. The devil told you that your family would die on drugs, but GOD said not so. Beloved, I don't know what you are going through, but my only words for you are believe and live. The storm you are going though, you will survive it. And all you have to do is decide that you want to survive it. Understand this man had been sitting at the foot of this pool for years, but all GOD wanted to know was if he wanted to be healed. Beloved, some of you have been waiting for a long time by your very own pool, and CHRIST wants to know: Do you want to be healed? Will you be healed? If your answer is yes, then pick up your bed and walk! Be HEALED! Beloved, the time for waiting for a miracle is over, you are the miracle. If you are waiting for a break-through, start walking like you already have the breakthrough! If you are waiting for your praise report, praise HIM like you already have the report. The word for this week is live. You will live through your depression! You will live through your family members' deaths! You will live through the drugs! You will live through alcoholism!

You will live through the recession! You will live through unem-ployment! You will live and not die. I don't have anything else for you beloved. I don't have a prophecy! I don't have a cloth to lay on you that will make it all better! I don't need a seed offering. All I have is the word of GOD, and the word from GOD is "be made whole". Move into your healing. You don't have to wait any longer, you just have to believe, because GOD has already declared that you will live and not die. So, I challenge you to start walking in that life. You are not your situation, because your situation is death, but you are life. Beloved, believe and LIVE!

Be Blessed Beloved.
Cloyed S. Brown, Jr.

Cloyed Brown is a minister and an empowerment speaker with a passion for helping and encouraging people through the word of God. Presently, he serves as a Minister for Renewing Life Church located in Raleigh, North Carolina and within the Life Center Fellowship of Interdependent Churches and Ministries. Cloyed is an alumnus of Park University, with a degree in Social Psychology. Cloyed presently resides in Cary, North Carolina with his wife LaTisha and son Aiden. He is a proud member of Kappa Alpha Psi Fraternity, Inc.

YOUR START DOES NOT DETERMINE YOUR FINISH

Dear Brother,

As an African American male, I've experienced a lot in my nearly 54 years of life. I've chronicled some of those moments over the next few pages. They capture portions of my life and times growing up black in America. It is my hope that you will enjoy learning about my journey, in hopes that it will inspire yours.

To my younger brothers, yes, you are growing up in a different time. A time when achievements are looked upon as positive developments worth celebrating. You are growing up in a time where life's struggles have all nearly been fought. You grow up in a time where with hard work, determination, that inner drive and with the correct skillset, you can reach just about any goal and desire you set out to achieve. Just as short as 30 years ago, reaching for the stars was much more difficult. During the formative years of my late teens and early twenties, which was in the mid to late 1980's, it was customary for African Americans to not even be considered for jobs or even be seen for an interview. The system was stacked against us. If you didn't know someone, or have a direct connection, you were shut out. I have given a tremendous amount of gratitude to my family, community, teachers, church members, ethnic groups and associations amongst others for helping pave the way for my generation. The adage that it took a village to raise a youth was so true. It took a village approach to make things happen; to give me opportunities to improve myself in various disciplines. So many people paved the way for me with their work ethic, voice, time, and their desire to see things change for my generation.

I proudly honor those who went before me as well as those who helped me get my start. I take it upon myself to honor those who provided a pathway for me. During high school I didn't take my education seriously. I didn't study as I should. Basically, my performance could have been described as lackluster. I had a teacher who said something to me that hurt like crazy, but it was effective in inspiring me. My high school music teacher, Angelo Holman, pulled me aside after class one day and said that I was not going to amount to anything because of my attitude and lack of determination. It hurt a lot hearing that sort of criticism. It was like being hit with a baseball bat squarely in the head. But I used it as a motivational tool.

I eventually decided to go on to college in the fall of 1984. I was accepted into East Carolina University, but my admission required me to take some general college courses that I should have taken and passed in high school. I was considered a student on probation. I did go on to improve my standing in school to the point where I was able to declare a major and be accepted into the School of Social Work. I remember earning a 4.0 in my senior year and being sent a letter from the Chancellors' office acknowledging my accomplishment. I went on to graduate from East Carolina University in May 1989 with a bachelor's degree. After graduation, I had to look for a job, but nothing would come easy. I had even considered heading to the military to get my start. But my dad called in some favors to help me get a chance at a job with the state of North Carolina.

I was later hired as a correctional officer in late 1989. I stayed in that job for about 6 months. Back in the 1980's and 90's, it was said to many, that a job with the state of North Carolina was a very good investment because of the opportunities for advancement it presented and the benefits that you were given. Thus, the second job I had was a Juvenile Court Counselor in the 8th judicial district (Wayne, Lenoir and Greene counties). I was recommended for this position by a local, black attorney, who was pushing for the juvenile justice community to hire African Americans into the system due to 75 percent of those served in the 3-county region being African American youths. So, in 1990 I was hired as the first African American Juvenile Court Counselor in the 8th judicial district in North Carolina. The words and actions of a local attorney opened another door for me.

I knew my work ethic and performance would be instrumental in helping diversify the workforce for the future. I was determined to make the process for bringing on more African Americans to be easier and smoother than what I encountered. While I was in the Juvenile Court Counselor position, the number of African Americans employed in the district went from none in 1990 to 7 out of 17 positions in 1995. So, we had tremendous growth in having African Americans employed and working with the at-risk youth population in the 3-county region. During my time as a Juvenile Court Counselor, one of my fellow co-workers asked me to attend a meeting of the local Jaycees. I eventually joined the organization. The Goldsboro Jaycees were considered a junior member and an extension of the local chamber of Commerce. The organization did a lot of work throughout the community. There were only 5 African American members out of about 60 members. The hard work and projects completed in the community led to me being elected as the first African American person to hold a leadership position in the Goldsboro Jaycees organization. During my tenure, I helped secure and direct some programs and services into the minority community. The exposure and work with the Goldsboro Jaycees led to my being selected by my supervisor at Juvenile Services to sit on a panel that helped establish Communities in Schools in the Wayne County School System.

All throughout my career I've taken the opportunity to help get other African Americans get involved in their respective communities. Some decided to provide mentoring, others helped with employment advice and coaching, while some took to being community activists. We as successful citizens must give back and share our experiences with the youth of today. The idea of "to whom much is given, much will be required" is that we are held responsible for what we have been given. When we have been blessed, be it with talents, wealth, or knowledge, it is expected that we use what we have to glorify God and to benefit others. It is up to your generation to continue to make sure the roads of the future are paved with equal opportunities for minorities and those who are disadvantaged. The one thing that complicates the process is that it seems the youth of today don't want to work hard or put forth the time and effort to succeed. They feel they are entitled to get what they want when they want it. There is a general disregard for the process or putting forth a timeline with good work ethic and habits. Some feel they should be able to start out at the top, choose which policies and procedures to follow and disregard those they don't like. Some do not like to even receive helpful criticism. I remember in my early years, I would listen and soak up all the helpful advice I received from older workers or adults I admired. I was thankful for the coaching and mentoring that was offered to me. I knew I had to crawl before I attempted to walk. I knew I had to take my time and gain experience before other opportunities would come my way. I want to see youth accept the advice and coaching provided. No one is trying to hold them back; we want them to excel. But you must have the right attitude to receive and take advantage of helpful coaching.

In 2009, I felt like my life had stagnated and had hit a plateau. I needed more, so I decided to pursue an advanced degree. This was not an easy decision because I had not been in school for more than 20 years, plus the cost for that education would not be cheap. In 2009 I enrolled in Walden University and graduated in 2011 with a Master in Public Administration. The master's degree opened the door for me to be able to apply and be hired for the job of Regional

Social Work Supervisor with the Department of Public Safety, Juvenile Justice Division. In this position, I was able to sit in on numerous interviews and eventually hire some very talented people. A majority of those hired just happened to be minorities and most were very happy to have been the chosen candidate. It warms my heart to know that as my career has just about run its course, I was able to give back to the community; as so much had been given to me many years earlier.

It is my hope that you were able to learn something from my journey. Of all the items within this letter, please remember:

Believe in yourself

You do not have to end how you started. You can achieve!

Always be willing to reach back and help your brother along the journey

Go as far as you can go

I remain optimistic that the future continues to show improvement for minorities. The future job and career options are limitless. We as a people will only be held back by our own limitations. Please stay focused and remember to keep your eyes on the prize.

David Kornegay

David Kornegay is a native of Raleigh, NC. He earned his Bachelor of Science Degree from East Carolina University and a Master of Public Administration from Walden University. He retired after working 30-years in the Health & Human Services Field. He currently volunteers as a mentor and coach for young professionals. He has received numerous awards and recognition as a public servant for the state of North Carolina.

DON'T FORGET YOUR CHARGER

Dear Brother,

We live in a world and a time where everything thrives off power. Without power, things in this world operate in a flatline mode. Recently, I upgraded cellphones, and while I was becoming acclimated to my new phone, I thought of all the cellphones that I have had throughout the years. I've noticed that out of all the cellphones I've had, they were all great phones. And when charged, they provided great service. However, after a while, they needed to be plugged up in order to keep providing the adequate service needed. At night, when we get ready for bed, one of the things that we do is make sure that our cellphones are plugged up in order to receive the charge that is needed for the next day. Many of us, when we start off our day, we take our cell phones off the charger and we notice that they are fully charged and ready to go. But some take it a step further and grab our chargers when we leave home. We even have car chargers now. We take them with us to our destination because at some point and time we are expecting our phones to lose power. Because of this, we are prepared to charge our phones so that we won't lose juice.

Just as our phones need to be recharged, so do our lives. We all need to be recharged from time to time. I'm sure that if I were to give you a microphone, you could say that the way has not always been easy, and perhaps, there have been sleepless nights. I'm sure you could say that your power runs low after facing the storms of life, many times, to only run out. Sometimes we have to confess to the Lord sometimes that we need to be recharged. We must rely on the Lord as our source of power when our power runs low.

Our phones only work for a certain amount of time before they need to be recharged. Our lives are the same way. There is only so much we can take or encounter before we need recharging. In 2009, my aunt bought me a Dell laptop as I prepared to go off to college. I still have this laptop today. It has gotten old, but now, it won't stay on without being hooked up to the power supply. As soon as the power supply is unplugged, it cuts off. Many of us have become like my laptop. As soon as we are unplugged from our power supply, we immediately cut off and quit working. I can personally relate to my laptop. Without my power supply, I would lose my mind. Without my power supply, I would not be able to function from day to day. Without my power supply, I would have given up a long time ago. Without my power supply, I would have thrown in the towel. I would be like a ship without a sail. I have concluded that I must be connected to my power supply at all times. That's the reason that when the church doors are open, I've got to be there. I cannot afford to hit and miss. I need my power, so I won't flatline. I've got to talk to my power source periodically throughout the day. It is necessary for me to have my charger with me at all times.

If I did not or do not carry my power supply with me at all times, I would be out of control. I would cuss some folks out. I would be lost in my way of thinking. I would be lost in my way of talking. I would be lost in my way of living. I would be lost in my way of being. I would probably be tricked into taking my own life. I would be outside of the will of God, which would cause me to be out of the ark of safety. We all should be able to say that having the right power is important. With having the right power comes the wisdom that we cannot rely on our own strength and power, but the power of God. The psalmist declares in Psalm 8, *"When I consider the heavens, the work of your fingers, the moon and the stars which you have set in place, what is mankind that you are mindful of them; human beings that they care for them?"* This is the question David could not help but ask, letting us know that although man appears to matter only a little, God has crowned him to have dominion over all creation and over all living things. We must recognize that we are created by God and are important to Him.

In Psalm 8, as David began to praise the majesty of God, he realized a great truth. He realized that God didn't make any junk and that God has made him a little lower than him; pretty high on the ladder, making him the ruler of all the earth, and has crowned him with glory and honor. This lets us know that our God is powerful, and if we would recharge ourselves with Him (because He is the source of power), He will grant us the power to have dominion over our circumstances. We must rely on His power to abide in us.

In Numbers 11:21-22 you will find the people of Israel whining about how good life had been in Egypt. They had eaten all the "manna casserole" that they could stand; they were craving the fish, the cucumbers, the melon, and the spices from Egypt. When Moses pleaded with the Lord, he was told that the people would have meat for a whole month. Moses found that hard to believe, seeing the multitude that was before him and a lack of resources. In v.21 and 22, *"Here am I among 600,000 men on feet and you say I will give you meat to eat for a whole month. Would you have enough if flocks and herds were slaughtered for them? Would you have enough if all the fish in the sea were caught for them?"* Apparently, Moses forgot that God was and is a mighty God. The same God that sent the plagues in the sea. His struggle was not of how good God was in the past, but that he cared. That he could and would help and deliver him out of this particular situation. The Lord's response was short. His response was "are the Lord's arms too short?" Did Moses believe that God was able to handle this?

If we were to be honest with one another, our questions would be "do we think God is able to handle our situation and bring us through?" This question is also asked for those who are trying to rebuild, whether through tragedy, death, divorce, or any other devastating loss. Those who have been trailing a road of sin and trying to turn their lives around; those who are trying to put a marriage back together after months and years of conflict. You feel like you are trying to put the pieces of a jigsaw puzzle together with a million pieces while wearing kitten mittens. This question is asked by those who are dealing with unforgiveness and trying to forgive when you don't see signs of true repentance or sorrow from the other person's heart whom they are trying to forgive. Not only do we find it difficult or as a challenge to trust in God's power (even though He has a great track record) in our personal and family lives. If we are truly rooted in the word of God, we can forgive when we feel like we cannot. We will be able to survive in life when we feel like we are sinking. We will be able to overcome sin when we feel like we don't have the strength to overcome. The God who created the heavens and the earth is working through us, and He has all power. He provides the power, but we must provide the willingness. That's why Paul prayed that believers would know God's power; incomparable great power within us. To the working of His mighty hand and mighty strength which was exerted in Christ as He was raised from the dead and seated in the heavenly realm. The Prophet Isaiah reminds us that in contrast to God's sovereignty and His greatness that the nations are as a drop of a basket and the small dusk of the balance. In other words, before this mighty God, the nations are nothing at all. This lets us know that God is all powerful, so why not connect yourself to the one who has all power? Isaiah declared in Chapter 40 that *"the Lord is the everlasting God, the creator of the ends of the earth; he*

does not faint, nor grow weary; his understanding is unsearchable;
he gives power to the faint and to them that have no might, he in-
creases strength. Even youths shall faint and grow weary and shall
utterly fall, but they that wait on the Lord shall renew their strength.
They shall mount up on wings as an eagle. They shall run and not
be weary, they shall walk and not faint."

Today if you are feeling dirty, because you can't imagine the
power of God to clean up your life, I am writing to tell you to look to
His power. If you're fighting a losing battle with addiction, with
drugs, with alcohol, with morality, with pride, with anger, I write
this letter to tell you to look to God for His strength. Are you weary
of trying to put your life back together after being abused, after being abandoned, after being attacked? I write this letter to tell you
today that you ought to fix your eyes on the one who called the
world into existence. Jehovah is not an abstract God. Jehovah is not
a distant God. Jehovah is not a silent God. He's not a fearful God.
But He's the one who called all things into existence. God, the victorious warrior. The One that conquered the forces of evil through
his son at the cross. The Lord of all who dwells within His people,
with His spirit. He's Jehovah Jireh – the Lord that will provide. Jehovah Rophe – the Lord who heals – Jehovah Shammah – the Lord
is always there – the Shalom – He is our Peace. El Shaddai – God
all significant.

I write this letter to let someone know to not be like Moses or the
children of Israel. Don't ever underestimate the power of God. The
children of Israel had become unhooked to the power supply. And
for that reason, they began to have selective amnesia. They began to
talk silly, they began to walk silly. They began to think silly. But
the Lord had to remind them that there was a consequence when
you're no longer hooked up to the power supply. I write this letter to
let you know that you've got to stay charged up. We've got to stay
hooked up to the power supply. I'm reminded of one of the great
hymns of the church:

Just ask the Savior to help you; comfort, strengthen and keep you.
He is willing to aid you. Jesus will carry you through.

This letter is to encourage you to stay connected to the power supply. The Lord's power will carry you through. His power will bring joy in the midst of sorrow, lift up a bowed down head, bring strength to your brokenness, stand with you, and fight for you. You're never alone because the Lord's power is with you. **GET CONNECTED** to the power supply.

Rev. Devin D. Paylor

Rev. Devin D. Paylor is a native of Roxboro, NC. He is a highly sought-after Speaker and Gospel Recording Artist. He holds a Bachelor of Arts Degree in Mass Communication with a concentration in Public Relations from Saint Augustine's University. He is currently pursuing a Master of Divinity from Shaw University. He is currently the Senior Pastor of Quinn Chapel AME Church. He is a gifted psalmist, composer, director, and two-time recording artist with the Instruments of Praise Mass Choir. He is the proud father of the joy of his life, Nicholas Isaiah Cates. Devin is a proud member of Kappa Alpha Psi Fraternity, Inc.

HISTORY MAKERS

Dear Brother,

Do you realize that you are more valuable than all the diamonds, in all the stores and mines throughout the world? Our skin tones come in a variety of shades; and just as precious priceless stones vary in color, their value does not diminish and neither does yours depending on the tone of your skin.

Growing up as a young boy in Cowpens, South Carolina, I wish that someone would have shared some important life lessons with me. The first of which is: don't let anyone devalue your self-worth or self-esteem. You see, we all have been fearfully and wonderfully made in the image of God (Psalms 139). And anything He made, was good. There will be days that you will have to be your greatest cheerleader. Let your light shine and radiate from the inside, so that it cast light into every dark place that you may encounter.

Secondly, do not suffer in silence. You are a voice in this world, and you deserve to be heard. If you are facing obstacles in your life, seek guidance, wisdom and instructions from those that have traveled the road you are on. It is never ok for anyone to disrespect your body or try and manipulate your mind. If you feel violated in any way, tell a teacher, a police person or a trusted family member. If you need help, seek out those resources. It is ok to see a counselor or therapist… it is better than ok, it is lifesaving.

Lastly, it is ok to cry. Often, we are told: "real men don't cry." That is one of the biggest lies that has ever been constructed. Emotions are the seat of the soul. Emotions are at the core of our being. We express emotions every day in some shape or form. A sense of accomplishment, earning good grades, excelling in sports, the death of a loved one and even the first heartbreaking relationship are all examples of emotions. So, if you must, cry to relieve pressure from your soul, but wipe your eyes and wash your face, because there is still much work for you to do.

While growing up, I missed out on some years with my father. Those missing years were so vital, that it strained the later years of our relationship. It made me take a good look at myself and realize how differently I would parent my children someday. I would look forward to dropping them off at college for the first time or hearing the excitement in their voices as I wished them a happy birthday. I know the importance of having a constant presence in the lives of my children. Fathers teach sons how to treat their wives and lead their families. And they teach their daughters what kind of treatment to expect from a real man. A real man is not defined by the number of women that he has "pulled", rather a real man is defined by his character and how he conducts himself when he thinks that no one is looking at him. I knew then and fully understand now that any man can be a daddy, but a real man will be a father to his children.

My brother, do you realize that you are making history each day. There has never been one of you in the world and guess what? There will never be another one of you ever again. Even if you have an identical twin, you are still different in so many ways. You are an original masterpiece. Do not take a single day for granted, because the next day or moment is not guaranteed for any of us. Time is precious, and once wasted, it cannot be recovered. Always remember that everyone has value and should always be treated with respect. Saying please and thank you will take you far in life.

Listen, I love you brother, because we are brothers. You are a part of my history and I celebrate the king in you. You are a thread in a rich fabric that makes us all unique. Yet it also makes us the same; within the same breath. I pray the blessing of the Lord overtakes you in every area of your life and that everything you set out to accomplish prospers. Use every opportunity that is presented to you to make a difference and stand firm on the fact that you are a priceless masterpiece, simply waiting to be discovered.

Respectfully submitted in Brotherly Love,
Derrick Wood

Derrick Wood is a native of Spartanburg, SC and a graduate of Lander University and Webster University. Derrick is an active member of his church in several capacities and is an active financial member of Phi Beta Sigma Fraternity, Inc. Derrick is employed as a social worker in foster care and loves impacting the lives of the families and children that he supports. Derrick is married and loves sharing life and experiences with his wife Tiesha.

GET UP

Life is not easy
You must get up and make a way
Get up and face another day
Sometimes it's going to be rough
But you've got to keep moving forward
I know God will make a way

Dear Brother,

GET UP! It's time to stop hiding behind the pain of your history. It's time to stop making excuses. It's time to stop waiting on your dreams to magically appear without sweat equity. It's time to get up and push forward.

Life is not easy! There will be some challenging times and painful moments. You will have seasons of happiness and sadness. You will find yourself at a standstill and wonder will my dreams ever become a reality. In those moments, you must get up and face another day. Each day awards a new opportunity to go after your goals. But you must be willing to at least **GET UP.**

Growing up as the son of the legendary Rock and Roll Hall of Fame inductee, Edward Patten of Gladys Knight and The Pips, many believed that my dreams and goals would be easy to achieve or that my life would be filled with fame and glamour. The reality is, I could not live in my father's shadow. He taught me that I had to create my own identity and goals; that life would not always be filled with fame and glamour. I still had to endure the same challenges and fight the same battles as every other Black Man. I often faced hatred, discrimination, and pain. At times I had to work extra harder than my counterparts. My goals often seemed impossible to accomplish and many times, I wanted to throw in the towel. However, each day, I would get up and try again. And because of that, today I stand as a R&B Recording Artist, Actor, and Motivational Speaker. I made the decision to not live in my dad's shadow, but I listened to his guidance and followed my own path.

Guess What? You can do the same. You can accomplish and achieve your goals. In order to do this, you must develop your own path in life. Having mentors and learning from them is a great thing, but you must apply what is learned to establish your own journey to what success is for you. You must also accept the fact that that life is not easy, you will face some challenges, you will have some dark days, and you will often feel like giving up. However, daily you must be tenacious and **GET UP** and keep moving forward. And always remember that God will make a way.

Brother, the stage is waiting on you...**JOIN ME!!**

Edward Teyamo Patten

Edward Teyamo Patten, is a native of Detroit, Michigan. He is a dynamic vocalist and is no stranger to the music business. He has been singing since the tender age of 5 years old. He established his roots singing in the church. Patten has had the privilege of opening for such noted acts as India Arie, Outkast, and Bobby Womack, as well as headlining at Atlanta's own, Sweet Merissa's. His voice is one that will move you and capture your ear.

YOU ARE GREATNESS

To My Dear Black Brother,

This letter is meant to encourage ALL my black brothers, no matter your age, background, current or previous situations. No matter what they say about us or what obstacles we may face, WE are Kings and are full of greatness!

I want you to take a close look in the mirror. Tell me what do you see? What do you think of yourself? Don't admire your looks, features or say that I need to trim this or cut that; but instead, see yourself as confident, a focused leader, a protector, a provider. Say to yourself: I AM MORE THAN ENOUGH! I AM FEARFULLY AND WONDERFULLY MADE! Say it with meaning and authority to yourself over and over every day until it becomes part of who you are!

Never let anyone tell you what you can't do because of your race. Never use your race as an excuse! In fact, your race is what makes you unique and consequently, well equipped to do anything! When I look at my brothers, I see bright futures and great potential for success, brothers who are pushing the limits, creating new standards and reaching new levels! Challenge yourself to do more than you ever could imagine and to be the very best at whatever you do! Don't be afraid to be great! However, you must know that reaching that success doesn't happen overnight; instead it takes constant work, adjustments, and a great deal of sacrifice to reach and maintain. Anything worth having is worth working for! You too can dream BIG and reach all that GOD has for you!

Remember, as black men we have a responsibility to always commit to learning, growing, improving, pursuing excellence and sharing knowledge with others. Keep my words of encouragement from this letter and other letters from this book. Reach back to share your knowledge and experiences with younger generations. Take the time and effort to make a positive impact by investing in another brother, your family, the local community and the extended community throughout the world. I am my brother's keeper!

I speak life into your future! May the rest of your days be filled with strength, inspiration, encouragement and motivation to continue BLACK EXCELLENCE!

Forever your brother,
Devon Johnson

Devon Johnson is a native of Bishopville, SC. He earned his Bachelor of Science degree in Business Administration in Marketing and Management from the University of South Carolina. He is a highly sought-after Marketing Professional and Strategic Planner. Throughout his career, Devon has worked in collegiate and professional sports for USC Gamecocks, Atlanta Braves, Lowe's, Chick-fil-a and many other prestigious organizations. He is currently employed with Aflac Insurance. He enjoys mentoring and coaching others to fulfill their dreams.

INVEST IN THE LIFE YOU DESIRE

Dear Brother,

One of the few things I tell young, black adolescents is to enjoy your journey; not only the destination. A lot of people get disturbed by their current situation, and it becomes difficult for them to see beyond those barriers or parameters. Positive affirmation, or manifestation, is without a shadow of a doubt real. I witnessed it throughout my life and through the lives of those that have been a part of my journey. I remind people that it doesn't happen overnight, but if you put in the work, you will see fruits of your labor in due time. Also, it is important to have a visual (outline) or an individual (mentor) that you see doing exactly what you want to do. The goal is to observe and study their moves and try as close as possible to mirror them, of course, with your own sense of style and originality. There's nothing new under the sun, but no two people do things the exact same way. Invest your man-hours. It's no different than the way people play video games or recite music lyrics. Most people only receive the bare minimum award because they put in the bare minimum during, what may be called, their apprenticeship stage. Lastly, remember that this process will not be easy. If it were easy, everybody would be doing it and would receive praise for their achievements. If you take this approach, you will not have to worry about faking it until you make it because people will see the raw, untapped potential in what you're doing. In other words, "If everybody stays in their lanes, there will be no wrecks".

Charles Ashley, Jr.

Charles Ashley Jr. is a Filmmaker/Music Producer raised in Gastonia, currently living in Raleigh, NC. He has created visuals on a variety of media platforms from advertising campaigns to magazine editorials, talent branding, books, music videos and films. Charles is a graduate of North Carolina Central University where he earned a Master of Social Work Degree. He is a proud member of Kappa Alpha Psi Fraternity, Inc.

EMBRACE YOUR LIFE'S
DETOURED ROUTE

Dear Brother,

Life, at occasions, has taken us for a ride or two wherein we were not prepared for them mentally. Moreover, they may have occurred during the times we presumed we had a grasp on our lives. Probably in our emotions, finances, relationships, businesses, ministries, etc., we've all undoubtedly approached a detoured construction zone in our life. Detours are defined as, "a deviation from a direct course: a roundabout way temporarily replacing part of a route."

When we think of detours, we undeniably become aggravated and think of how we are being inconvenienced. However, I would like to offer a different way of viewing a detoured route. I am going to support you by consciously training your mind to think more positive and live the empowering and wealthy life you were created to live.

The beginning of conquering our detour, is to simply acknowledge the feeling. Also, healing is imperative, as we allow ourselves to confront the pain, which is defined as an, "acute mental or emotional distress or suffering; trouble, care, or effort taken to accomplish something." There are three redefining principles that we must apply, if we are going to have a successful outcome.

Accept Reality: Acceptance doesn't necessarily mean that I agree with it, but that I do not walk in a delusional (deceiving YOURSELF) state of mind, which is a mental illness. Accepting reality is about recognizing what's within your control. When you can't control the situation, then you focus on controlling yourself.

Behave Productively: Accepting reality helps you manage your thoughts and regulate your emotions—which are key to productive behavior. The choices we make determine the outcomes of situations! Unproductive behavior, like complaining or throwing a pity party, will keep you stuck. Those behaviors will rob you of mental strength. When we are stuck in the middle of uncertainty, it's imperative to ask ourselves, "What can I do for myself in this, that's within integrity?"

Control Our Thoughts: Our minds can be our best asset or our biggest enemy. We should create a mantra that we repeat during tough times. Doing so can help quiet the negative chatter that threatens to drag us down. Building mental strength is like building physical strength. While you may not think about your mental muscle until you need it the most, a crisis isn't the best time to build mental strength.

It is imperative that we become liberated from any oppression. Self-inflicted oppression or that which has been placed upon our life by someone else. It is incomprehensible to fight and win an encounter if we are constrained in bondage.

Ideally, the enemy strikes our minds, because they know well that if our minds rest in hopelessness, delusion, confusion, and among other things, then we will become unhinged in every area of our lives.

Nonetheless, when we comprehend that favor suits us, then it will not only change the approach in which we contest, but it will also revolutionize our mind and that's when we launch into a sweat-less victory, while we encounter our life's detoured route.

Dr. Jesse Sanders, DFMT, NCC
Family, Marriage, and Relationship Therapist
Redefined LLC | www.iamredefined.org

Dr. Jesse D. Sanders is a nationally-recognized Therapist and Empowerment Life Coach with over 20 years of experience. He is the founder of Redefined, LLC., an organization that helps individuals, families, and organizations take a detour from life's construction zone to lead to a path of personal growth and opportunities. The innovative, limitless, no boundaries, motivational, minister, inspirational speaker, single father and co-parent father, has led individuals to find tenacity and strength to change their circumstances through positive self-inquiry and actions.

DEAR BROTHERS - MOVE!!!

*Let your forward momentum be powered
by the energy of your dreams.*

My Brothers,

This journey that we call life is not easy. Over the years, we all have had obstacles that have presented challenges to us emotionally, spiritually, and at times, physically. Sometimes it's hard to wake up in the morning to face another day, knowing that you have those challenges ahead. Know that your journey is unique. There is no other person on this planet who has experienced or is experiencing the identical challenges that you have; however, I write you today to tell you that no matter what has happened, success is possible and true happiness is achievable by harnessing the energy of your dreams.

One of the earliest challenges that I remember encountering in life happened was when I was about five years old. My parents had enrolled me in a swimming class. At one point, all the kids had to line up on the diving board to take turns jumping into the pool. As I stood in line and watched each kid in front of me jump off into the water, I became more and more anxious. My hands began to sweat, my heart raced and the butterflies in my stomach seemed to flutter making me feel nauseous. It was finally my turn. I reached the edge of the board and froze in terror. In my mind I knew that I could swim enough to survive the jump, especially since our instructors were in the water waiting to assist us, but my body was completely frozen. I remember the kids behind me yelling for me to jump. Some kids were encouraging, telling me that I could do it and that there was nothing to fear. Other kids were laughing, because they found my crippling fear amusing. However, the kid directly behind me was impatient and felt that I was wasting everyone's time. All of a sudden, he pushed me off the edge of the diving board. At that point, everything seemed to happen in slow motion. I remember falling in feet first and going deep down under the water. My lungs began to tighten and the only thing on my mind was the fact that I was out of air and I needed to get to the surface so that I could breathe. Almost innately, I pushed off the bottom of the pool and began to glide to the surface. I still remember the relief I felt when I finally reached the surface and was able to take in my first breath of air. I remember the sense of accomplishment that I felt, not because I jumped off the diving board (because I was pushed), but because once I was in the water, I survived. When I think back on this moment in my life, I was never in any real danger because of the presence of instructors in the water. I use it as a metaphor for tackling all of life's challenges. Often, we find ourselves thrown into situations that terrify us, but by focusing on the end goal (our dream) and using its energy to power our momentum, we can succeed. This process does not just work for a scared five-year old at the bottom of a pool, it also works for every challenge that we face in our lives.

Inertia

Famed physicist, Sir Isaac Newton, created three laws of motion. The first law was inertia, which he defined as, "a property of matter by which it continues in its existing state of rest or uniform motion in a straight line unless that state is changed by an external force". In other words, nothing changes unless we change it. As a scared, five-year-old, running out of air at the bottom of a pool, I decided that breathing air was my greatest need in that moment. Although I was not totally responsible for my circumstance, because I was suddenly pushed into the water, it was my duty to survive. I did not waste time focusing on how unfair it was that a kid had pushed me in the water, because it was already done. I also did not sit on the bottom of the pool feeling sorry for myself. I could only concentrate on the next step: How to get to the top and breathe air again.

Sometimes in life we become distracted by past choices or the actions of others that resulted in our challenges. When presented with challenging obstacles in life, we cannot live in the past. We must quickly forgive ourselves and others for the choices that resulted in our current situation. Then we must quickly focus on our immediate goal of overcoming that obstacle. When I was underwater, all I wanted to do was get to the surface and breathe. Every action that I took after entering the water was directly related to that immediate goal. I'm sure at five years old, my swimming form was not perfect, but I made it to the surface and survived. Life works the same way. Give yourself space to make mistakes and to not be perfect and keep pushing forward towards your goals. A wise mentor once told me that mistakes do not stop success; only fear does. Do not let your fear paralyze you and stop your forward momentum. Imagine, had I stayed underwater and refused to move, I would have given out of air, taken in water, and possibly drowned. As Sir Isaac Newton showed us in his first law of motion, nothing changes if we don't change it.

F=ma

Newton's second law of motion is described as *F=ma* (Force equals mass times acceleration) or the vector sum of the forces on an object is equal to the mass of that object multiplied by the acceleration vector of the object. In other words, it's not just the force you use to move an object, but it is also the direction wherein you apply the force that affects the outcome. This law can also help us as we face challenging situations. When I was under water, I had assessed that the most efficient way to breathe air again was to push off from the bottom of the pool and use that momentum to swim straight up to the surface. Sometimes in life we do tackle challenges by capitalizing on the energy created by our goals, but we apply that energy in the wrong places. Under water, instead of using all my strength for one big push to the surface, I could have panicked and began to wildly kick and scream, which would have resulted in me taking on water and possibly drowning. I could have also tried swimming at an angle toward the perceived safety of the sidewall of the pool. But would I have had enough air to make it? When facing challenges, be sure to use your momentum in prudent ways to essentially work smarter and not so hard as to waste momentum.

Action/Reaction

Newton's third law of motion states that for every force in nature there is an equal reaction. Most commonly known explained as, for every action there is an equal and/or opposite reaction. Think of it like walking on a treadmill. As you try to walk and use your energy toward forward momentum, the belt on the treadmill rolls in the opposite direction. Overcoming life's challenges work the same way. Sometimes we can be so focused on facing the challenge head-on and use so much energy at once that we experience burn-out. Burn-out because we have not gotten enough sleep, we have not eaten the proper nutrition, or participated in activities that allow us to de-stress. Sometimes burn-out can cause our challenges to seem bigger than they are because we are simply exhausted. One solution to burn-out is attempting to live a balanced life, or a life within a state of equilibrium. You should make time for work, healthy living, sleep, and recreation. Only with a state of balanced equilibrium can we even begin to think clearly enough to properly assess our challenges and clear out our obstacles.

As a five-year-old, I didn't know about Sir Isaac Newton or how to apply his laws of motion to my daily life, but as an adult I apply his teachings to tackling challenging obstacles by understanding that nothing changes unless I change it. It's not just the energy I use to change a situation, I must also assess the proper placement of that energy. Finally, live in equilibrium by balancing work, healthy living, sleep, and recreation. In overcoming your challenges, you must never forget the goal (dreams) that you are trying to accomplish. Always remember to move and let your forward momentum be powered by the energy of your dreams.

Love and Light.
Roy N. Rasheed

Roy N. Rasheed is an educator with over twenty years' experience in higher education (counseling and student personnel services), K-12 music education, and private sector management. He holds a bachelor's degree from Valdosta State University and a master's degree from the University of Southern Mississippi. Roy considers mentoring, student development, and inspiring people to become the best version of themselves to be his personal mission. He is a musician, has a love for the Fine Arts and can be often found in attendance at area Arts events and workshops. He is a proud member of Alpha Phi Alpha Fraternity, Inc.

WALK THE ROAD

The world is oh so cold,
but there's warmth within your heart.
You are oh so bold,
but there's fear on where to start.
Your dreams are a bit too unreal they say.
Well show them how to live your dream today.
There's a roadblock.
Time to reroute.
Don't you ever stop,
never have a doubt.
Remember failure is but a lesson.
Never think it makes you the lesser.
The road is long, but don't stop now.
Keep your head up and walk it with pride.
Oh, I know they've gotten to the end of theirs, don't frown
We have to take ten steps for every one of their strides.
It's ok, the end is in sight.
Look! You've survived the fight!
Now the path for your children is clear
show them the way to get here.
BLACKMAN keep your head held high.
And never let it drop during any stride.

Jonathan A. Talley has been writing since he can remember. He currently resides in Washington, DC. He is a highly sought-after actor, spoken word artist, and emcee He is the proud father of three girls. He enjoys using his poetic voice to empower others.

HELP YOUR BROTHER

Dear Brother,

We have a national emergency!
Is history repeating itself–over and over and over again?
Are we doomed?
Is there hope?

Our youth have limited academic achievement. Drug abuse and crime has infested our communities. This should be a concern for all of us as Black Men. I write this letter to challenge each of you to deal with the issues of injustice and racism that are continuing to oppress our people. As a black minister, ministering to black people, I believe that black liberation is, at least in part, dependent upon the attitude and role that the Black Men assume in relation to it.

Before we blacks, as a people, were allowed to be identified with our families, we found refuge, healing, and love in our faith. Our families were destroyed. Our mothers and fathers, sisters and brothers, were sold from plantation to plantation. They were driven from one field to another and forced to breed like cattle. Our families were torn apart, educating our mind was not allowed, our businesses were crushed, but our faith helped us to endure the hard times. It is the nature of the Black Man to endure under persecution and make it through trials and tribulations. We must remember this today when we face challenges.

Let us remember that our fore parents did more with less money and less education, while today, we are doing very little with more money and more education. We need to go back to the old times and come together. The fight for freedom is still the first burden of the Black Man. We must work in unity with all our brothers. The low and the high, the young and the old, the rich and the poor, those who think they are sophisticated and those who know they are not . . . we should love and work together in harmony. Can you imagine the power if all black men stood side by side in unity and sung songs of freedom? Regardless if they are grammar school dropouts, college graduates, or Ph.D.'s! Can you imagine the impact we would have standing in unity against things that are hindering us as black men?

I would like for you to consider the role of Simon, found in Matthew: 27-32, he was a model of a man that supported, uplifted, and worked with his fellow brother. We will not get into a long argument about Simon's alleged blackness. Whether or not Simon was physically black, like you and I, is an open question. But for all practical purposes, Simon represented a Black Man's humanity. Simon was identified with an inspired segment of people. He was isolated. He was given no freedom of choice of whether or not to bear the cross. His manhood was not respected. Simon was compelled to be where Jesus was, because Jesus had decided to be where Simon was. Jesus had already decided to identify himself and his kingdom with Simon. Simon was black due to his identity. Jesus was black due to his own decision.

The cross was too heavy for Jesus to bear alone. The Roman soldiers began to search through the crowd trying to find somebody to help Jesus bear the cross. None would volunteer. The Jews wouldn't touch it because they were too religious. The Romans wouldn't touch it because they were too proud. The soldiers wouldn't touch it because they were too powerful. The Greeks wouldn't touch it because they were too philosophical. The Asians wouldn't touch it because they were too insecure. The Europeans wouldn't touch it because they were too arrogant. His friends wouldn't touch it because they were too scared. And his enemies wouldn't touch it because they didn't care. They kept on searching through the crowd, trying to find somebody who would get under the weight of the cross. Finally, they spotted a Black face in a sea of White faces. They found the man whose muscles had been strengthened by years of forced labor. They found the man from Africa–Simon by name. He was a slave. He didn't want to do it. He also was angry and resentful, but they made him do it anyhow.

At first, he protested inwardly, but then he looked in the face of his strange partner on the other end of the cross. And he saw love, power, joy, mercy and compassion all wrapped up together in the face of Jesus Christ. Instantly, he accepted the cross. He did not ask what will happen to me if I bear the cross, but what will happen to the world if I don't bear it. Here I am at the center of history. If I don't bear it, the earth will be destroyed; the universe will go back to chaos. If I don't bear it, all my people will lose. The songs of Zion will never be sung. Preachers, the Gospel will never be preached.

In church, souls will never be saved, sinners will never be rescued, and the racist will never be reconciled. If I don't bear the cross, faith will go out of existence, love will turn to ashes, hope will die stillborn, and death will never lose its sting. The grave will lift up the victory.

If I don't bear it, the devil will never be defeated, the highway to heaven will become a dead-end street. If I don't bear it, darkness will rule over the light, hatred will prevail over love, the wicked will never cease from troubling, and the weary will never be at rest. Paul could never organize churches. America will never be established, schools will never be built, churches will never stand, and families will never be saved. So, I'll cherish... the old rugged cross... I will cling to the old rugged cross... and exchange it someday for a crown.

Simon was compelled into existence. To begin, Simon's verdict is to serve his own people because his people have no real hope of being genuinely accepted anywhere. Although we boast and brag about a black president, a Black mayor here and there, one Black Supreme Court justice, a Black U.S. Senator, a Black school superintendent, a Black this and Black that. Many Black Males are still experiencing police brutality, mass incarceration, unfair treatment, experiencing poverty, and dealing with adversity, etc. We, as Black Men, we must unify; we must serve our people and not ourselves to change the Face of the Black Man in America!

Dr. Kenny W. Rose

Dr. Kenny W. Rose is a native of Sumter, SC. He currently holds a Bachelor of Arts from Morris College, a Master of Arts Degree from South Carolina State University, and a Ph.D. from the Union Institute. He is a Licensed Independent Social Worker, Licensed Master Social Worker, and Certified Rehabilitation Counselor, which allows him to practice as a Psychologist. He is a life member of the NAACP and the Omega Psi Phi Fraternity, Inc. He is the Pastor and Founder of United Bible Way Church of Lancaster, Inc. Dr. Rose is married to Angela Fonta Johnson Rose and they are the proud parents of one son, Kendal DeAngelo Rose.

YOUR REAL IMAGE

Dear Brothers,

Let me begin by saying I see you... I feel you... I am you! My name is Frederick James and I'm from Durham, NC. I have a background in several different industries, manufacturing, engineering, insurance, long term care facility management and several entrepreneurial ventures. I grew up in mixed environments, one being urban and the other rural, neither racist, mean spirited, nor homophobic. Sure, people had their preferences, but they were nice to all people under any and every non-threatening circumstance. I grew up loving my family and they loved me, even if we didn't always agree. We respected our family unity as well as our own, unique individuality.

Yes, we are unapologetically individuals, but as I have discovered, undeniably indivisible. We are all members of the human family of which we identify our African American ancestry, heritage, existence, embodiment and image. Of those identifiers, I'd like to talk specifically about image. Images are visible "entities" that display form, shape, color and character. We live in a society where image is regarded as an important element of a person's life. It is often used to establish a person's position/value in a socioeconomic system that is embraced by the masses. Even though we are individuals, in this socioeconomic system, we are all looked at as the same.

And although we are indivisible, we have individual personalities, dreams and aspirations which create our own personal image. I am writing this letter to you so that you can consciously master the making of your individual, indivisible self. Which is to say, your unique expression in the whole of humanity. In this writing you will discover the superpower that you possess, which will become the foundation for you to create and cultivate an amazing life, your amazing life! This super power is found in your own, personal Self-Image: the way you see yourself.

Fact, no matter what anyone outside of you thinks about you, the most important principle and practice is the way you see and treat yourself. The way you see yourself will determine how you treat yourself and how you entreat yourself. Consider now how you see and how much value you see in yourself. Take a moment and quietly dig beneath the layers of your thoughts about the "real" you and determine where your thoughts about you and your value of yourself, your dreams, your abilities and inabilities, your strength and weakness, your self-confidence and lack of self-confidence, your courage and your fears. Where did these thoughts and valuations come from? You may discover, as most of us have, that your thoughts and valuations around many of these areas of your life are given to us by others, parents, family, friends and even the media. Additionally, another major contributor is the church, temple or synagogue in which family, friends and the media are engaged. Some of the common themes coming from these institutions center on the ills/evils that people in general are supposedly born with and possess until they ascribe to the teachings and the teacher of the specific religion. When you research the passages found in the religious books, you find that more principles point to the divinity of people rather than evil. For sure, people have done some bad things, but it doesn't warrant assigning every person with inherent evil, which in turn suggests to people that they are flawed from birth. This suggestion alone has encapsulated mass amounts of people, who look at themselves as "bad" people. People who need to be fixed. I sometimes hear parents, relatives and friends telling children that "they're bad" or "they're going to be bad". They speak as though one or two misbehaving acts can constitute being or becoming a "bad" person. The media outlets have and continue to promote negative images of African Americans, especially African American Males, through various types of video footage and audio soundtracks. On the other hand, the media promotes other "social norms" that suggest that African Americans, especially the males, are sub-standard and should be avoided. The news outlets heavily promote crimes committed by African Americans, especially the males. STOP! During all this chatter about how bad you are, YOU must STOP the chatter and speak to yourself. You must remind yourself that when you were conceived, the birth process involves hundreds of thousands to millions of little sperm cells travelling through to reach one destination and you are the one who made it! I used to think that the sperm cells were competing for the target, but I soon learned that the sperm were not competing totally. They were absolutely making sure that the fastest, strongest and most determined Sperm Cell would make it and all of those that fell behind enter the process of pushing and encouraging the fore-runner. Please hear and see this. When you were just a clot of water called sperm, you competed against hundreds of thousands to millions of others, just like you, in order to begin the fertilization process. You were the fastest, the strongest, and most coordinated out of hundreds of thousands to millions of beings just like you. You were born with energy to reach your destination and make the connection to move to the next level. YES, the fact that as a clot of water, you were able to not only reach the destination, but you were able to form a relationship with your counterpart at that time, the egg. This shows that you, in fact, do have the ability to form relationships and keep them! The fertilization process is not an overnight process. It takes the right conditions and commitment to complete the process and YOU completed it! Then after forming the new relationship and completing the marriage process, you fully emerged into the new being formed out of that union. You became "one" with your counterpart on that level and began the process of forming a new body. And you did all of this in a totally new environment, one where you and your surroundings became amazingly familiar with one another, to the point where you both worked together in cooperation to ensure that this miracle process was successful. And it didn't stop there! After the formation of your body and function of your body parts had come to term, you were pushed out into a new world where you had to learn a new language, live in a completely different environment, learn how to function and YOU DID IT! YES, with some help, of course, YOU did it! And now is the process of remembering the power that brought you to this place. Remember the millions of companions that you had pushing you and even seemingly competing with you to encourage you to run faster, jump higher, go the longer distance. Not only remember them in your thoughts but feel that that close comradery in your soul that comes from an inner feeling.

This is an inside job, and much of it will be carried out in silent contemplation of the words that I'm saying. Turn off the outer chatter. Power off all of the devices that distract you. Tell your significant other or friend to allow you a little space to sit in timeless silence so that you can reconnect and realign with your soul and your soul's power. The process of "Re-Membering" is the process of reconnecting the parts of you that make you invincible and always a winner. Yes, and no matter what anyone says, YOU are a WINNER. Your job is to identify with the winning power inside of you. Identify with the beautiful, the handsome, the cute, the attractive, or whichever suits you best, power within you. Feel your power surging up from within that will bring clarity to your thoughts and diminish any self-hate, self-doubt or self-sabotage. Find the clear image of the "real" YOU and see yourself as soulfully connected, humble, peaceful, powerful, resourceful, coordinated, refined, committed, loving, loyal, confident, goal oriented, beautiful, handsome, healthy, wealthy, well spoken, learned, cosmically connected, purposefully manifested, blessed, uplifted, supported, secured, celebrated, admired and perfecting soul that you really are in this life. Know this for sure and let no outside teachings, chatter, gossip, media or otherwise, sway YOU from these facts. Enjoy your amazing life as the Amazing YOU…your true Self-Image.

Frederick James

Frederick James is a native of Durham, NC. He is a graduate of NC State and NC A&T State Universities. He worked in manufacturing for three Fortune 500 companies as well as a local manufacturer. He played the piano for different churches and later became a Minister, then Pastor where he led a congregation for 10 years. While in college, he experienced an awakening that formed a coalition between religious beliefs, spiritual awareness and physical disciplines such as mathematics, chemistry, biology, physics and engineering. This journey has caused him to challenge many of his prior religious beliefs, mainly the beliefs about himself and others. Frederick has mentored many high school and college students and continues to do so in hopes that they may transcend the mundane and soar into the amazing possibilities that lies in each person. He has a passion for family and friends. His motto is, "Keep it real! Keep it relevant!"

GET FIT

Good Day Future,

I write "future", as in the new wave. By that, I mean you are destined to be a leader, whether you realize it or not. More to this story as we grow later on. My name is Antwaun Arnold, a proud "mama's boy" from Columbia, South Carolina. I mention proud with much emphasis and pride, because my mother, Jacklan James, raised me to become the man I am today. Growing up wasn't hard, but it was challenging. Challenging in a way that kept me thinking and wanting to do more to represent my family. You see, I don't use the fact that I grew up without my father as a crutch, rather I made it my fuel, to keep me ignited to achieve no matter what. As I grew, nothing meant more to me than to represent my family the best way I knew how, and that was through achieving, academically. I'm currently a Director for a non-profit organization that works with youth. Working with youth is both my passion and my purpose.

Think of life as a gym. Inside this gym there will be people trying to gain or lose weight. Weights are symbolic of the challenges we face. Take a moment to visualize yourself inside this gym. Your first instinct is to see what others are lifting around you and match or increase your weight according to theirs. Like many of us, we like to start where we think the majority of others are. However, unless you have had that experience, you cannot tell right away what you're able to handle. This is a common mistake, especially with us: men. We tend to compete by thinking we can handle more weight than the next person. Instead, the objective should be to first understand the motivation behind making the next person work hard. Now, having some experience with weights, I know first-hand it's a process built over time. No one walks out of a gym on their first day with their ideal image. In order to achieve this, you must work. You increase your weight to make gains. You work harder and increase reps to burn fat. Notice how this process works? It starts with you working. This is solely an independent strategy based on how much work you put in. Essentially, some are more dedicated than others. Start with developing short-term goals. Identify what it is that you want to accomplish. What do you want to achieve? What is your purpose?

I challenge you to walk in your purpose. Live your life determined and without fear of failure, for failure represents learning and experience of how to become better.

Be Strong!
Antwaun Arnold

Antwaun Arnold is a native of Columbia, Sc. He holds a Bachelor of Arts degree in Management Information Systems from the University of South Carolina and a Master of Science Degree in Human Behavior from Capella University, He is currently the Executive Director for Infinity Wake County. He has served as a youth advocate for over 20 years. He is Married to the love of his life, Eboni Arnold. They are the proud parents of Aubree Arnold. He is proud member of Kappa Alpha Psi Fraternity, Inc.

J. D w a y n e G a r n e t t

OUR "SECRET" IDENTITY

Dear Brother,

The complexity of our survival as black men is as murky and messy as the intricacies of our role in society. Because of social inequality, it is more challenging to gain or grasp an understanding of "who" we are and even more so, how are we to do it. By no means, do I claim to be a historian or sociologist; therefore, the intent of this writing is not to "educate" but to encourage you as my brother. Many believe that the present ideology of the African American male experience and culture is a direct response to slavery, institutional racism, and systematic discrimination. I must say, I largely agree because I understand that though we live in a post-slavery era, the damaging ideals, despite hopeful wishing, did not dissolve with the abolishment of slavery. Of course, there can be an argument of the various nuances that bleed into solitary instances, but my desire is not to go that in depth.

See, as an African American male, **"We are not who they think we are."** Each day, we must contend with the negative and positive effects of social constructs. Unfortunately, there are so many false narratives that have distorted the image of being a "Black Man" in America that we are forced to either eradicate or redefine, images such as uneducated, overly attitudinal, or aggressive. Not to mention, the constant fear of police brutality or unwarranted death. Though there is a stigma that considers African American males the "lesser" male, he is still a male and receives the benefit of being one, along with adhering to a forced definition of a "man." Therefore, I recognize that I may receive employment or financial opportunities based solely on my gender; if only I remember my place as a black male. With this, we must end the "chameleon complex" of "faking it 'til we make it." See, I understand that this is a survival technique for many of us as black men, but we must shift our mindset. We must stop settling for less than, embrace the light that is within us, learn to love ourselves, and realize that time is one of the most important gifts we have, and we cannot continue to waste it.

Giving up should never be an option. Often times, the "struggles of life" make us feel as if surrendering is the only option. No, if you want "better", then pursue it aggressively. No one should ever be content with settling. Settling opens the doors for commitment to failure, which has the ability to contaminate and destroy everything you've worked so hard to build. So, don't settle in your relationship, career, family, and/or faith. Though life has its share of difficulties, it should never be lived as "moments of regrets". Life should be enjoyable and rewarding. Surround yourself with positive people who understand your worth and have a vision for "greater". Whatever you do, don't SETTLE!

I wonder how many people really realize who's the light in all of this darkness. Do you realize that you are the light, and you were chosen to be so? You were charged to be this light. The scripture declares, "You are the light of the world. A city set on a hill cannot be hidden" (Matt 5:14). Your only responsibility is to be brilliant. If you study the history of this word, it means "to shine" or "shining". What shines other than light? All the answers that you are seeking, questions you may have, everything you are trying to be, everything you are trying to do, you will find the resolve when you discover who you really are. Your only responsibility is to SHINE, be that LIGHT and be BRILLIANT! Be who you really are. Stop trying to be anything else other than yourself. It is time to really start focusing on you. Be accountable to yourself ...be the LIGHT, I need you to SHINE.

Everyone has a crossroad to travel that typically rests on the intersection of purpose and identity. Unfortunately, neither can truly be accomplished without understanding self. Many assume that if we have achieved fulfillment, then we have automatically obtained purpose. I disagree with that whole theory because fulfillment means "accomplishment, achievement, realization, or completion". Fulfillment is mentioned as if it is a journey, when actually, it is the conclusion of one. This word clearly implies an ending of some sort. On the other hand, purpose is a term of position; meaning, "the reason for which something is done or created or for which something exists". Therefore, our purpose should be aligned with our reason for existing. This cannot happen if we are unaware of WHO we are. It is time to arrest purpose and seek. Enjoying or appreciating one's self should never feel like a task or planned event. There is nothing wrong with being spontaneous, yet intentional, with loving yourself. Often, we selflessly give to others while neglecting ourselves in the process. I fear that somewhere along the way, we have been taught that self-appreciation is socially abhorrent; when actually, it is quite despicable not to have some sense of self-worth or value. Oblige yourself in becoming reacquainted. When was the last time you really measured or assessed your happiness? When was the last time you really treated yourself to something special? You should make it a priority to have a "FUN-DAY" with yourself! Be mindful to celebrate those small and critical victories. You can't have a standard for others if you refuse to follow through with yourself. Break away from the "hustle and bustle" of the day and love you! Get to loving and throw yourself a party.

Time is probably one of the most valuable things that we are gifted. I cannot help but wonder how many of us are either wasting time or investing it. See, time is one of those things we cannot control, but we can control what we do with it. We can fumble through life with many failed attempts, or we can choose to do the things we excel in, for instance, being ourselves. Let's face it, we know exactly what we are purposed to do. It is that one thing that constantly gnaws at us when we try to do anything contrary. Because time is so precious, it should be used on those things that we consider precious. Of course, the choice is yours. You can either accept it or reject it. Living a life of refusal and self-rejection would definitely be a hindrance toward self-awareness and actualization. Free yourself from the burden of frustration and find resolve in your path of fulfillment. You owe it to yourself to be you. Stop wasting time on those things that are ineffectual. Rather, invest in those things that are of great value. Remember, we cannot control time, but we can control what we do with it.

Brothers, at times, it may appear as if we are walking our last mile and all hope is gone. However, our journeys have prepared us for transition, elevation, and repositioning within our society; most importantly, for the purpose to take our place in society. We must continue to journey on.

In Brotherly Love,
J. Dwayne Garnett

J. Dwayne Garnett is a native of Augusta, GA, who has resided in Columbia, SC for many years prior to moving to Fuquay-Varina, NC. He's an educator, author, and speaker, who's extremely passionate about serving others. Though community empowerment brings him an immense amount of joy, nothing compares to the feeling he receives from being the husband to the amazingly beautiful, Lalita Garnett and father of two adorable daughters, Lailani and Lanaila. As a family, they are committed to promoting unity, love and random acts of kindness through their non-profit, Love Is A Parable. Find out more at loveisaparable.com. He is a proud member of Phi Beta Sigma Fraternity, Inc.

CHOOSE YOUR ROYALTY

Dear Phenomenal African American King,

What an honor and privilege it is to write you this letter, to infuse you with much needed encouragement for your sojourn on this life's journey and to express my appreciation for who and what you are and have always been. Yes, I say encouragement because as quiet as it is kept, you have those days and moments when you not only feel but are truly despaired, discounted, and disenfranchised by the very persons and systems that are supposed to strengthen, serve, and secure you. Typically, you go about your day most often without communicating the deeply rooted fears, anguish, and even insecurities, due in no small part to the expectations that society has placed upon you. The expectations to be strong, to be invincible, to not allow inward oppressions to become outward expressions. Yet, my brother, throughout history you have always been a stalwart phenomenon for your family and community. Your resolve of resilience has maintained families and communities. That is because you were divinely designed to be of, what I call, the "Moses Factor."

Moses, according to historical and geographical accounts, was of African descent, a Hebrew born in the southern part of Egypt known as Goshen, dark skinned, and had a speech impediment. Even Moses's birth was under oppression as he was hidden as a 2-month old

baby by his mother to avoid being killed under the authority and or-
ders of Pharaoh. However, because of God's divine purpose for
Moses's life and for His people, Moses was found by Pharaoh's
daughter and reared in royalty despite his Hebrew origin. However,
as a young, matured adult, Moses saw the oppression of his Hebrew
people and stood up to the oppression by the Egyptians by defending
a slave and slaying the oppressive Egyptian guard. As a result of his
actions, he was forced to leave his place of royalty and relegated to
the land of Midian where several years later he had a divine encounter with God at a burning bush and received his assignment to free
his people from the subjugation of the Egyptians.

You may ask, what does all of this have to do with you my brother? Well, I'm glad you asked. There are at least 4 principles that are
directly related to the "choices" that Moses made that parallel the
choices you, my brother, have made, make today, and will make tomorrow:

**Because of God's "design" for his life, Moses chose to refuse
to allow himself to be defined and ultimately confined by the
opinion of other people.** The message here is be your authentic self
and walk in the truth of who you are. Too often as African American
men, we tend to conform to who or what people think we should be
in order to gain acceptance or to get ahead. However, I challenge
you to walk and live in the who and what God has designed you to
be and do. By doing so, whatever your needs may be will be provided. Conforming to something you're not means you're acting out a
role.

Moses chose short-term pain for long-term gain. My brother,
you've heard of the term "no pain, no gain." Too many people want
what they want, when they want it, and how they want it. It's what I
call the "microwave mentality." Delayed gratification will always
yield a greater value. Just as seeds do not germinate and grow overnight, so too does everything good in life. It takes time and process.
Moses chose to voluntarily live in the desert of Midian for 40 years

rather than the palace of Egypt, because his morals and values were in the right place–resisting injustice. Just as so many of you could have immediate wealth and power by giving into the waywardness of oppressive people and systems, you choose to stand against it, even if it means temporarily being without some of the better things in life. In your family and in your community, sacrifice is necessary as a leader. But the end result will always be empowering to you and to others. As a result of Moses resisting injustice, he was chosen by God to return to the place of the oppression to help end the injustices by ultimately leading the children of Israel out of the land of Egypt, and into the Promised Land. Moses chose God's PURPOSE over popularity, God's PEOPLE over pleasure, and God's PEACE over possessions.

Moses chose to live by faith and not by fear. I look at our ancestors, those who were physical slaves, but spiritually free; the civil rights activists who were physically wounded and imprisoned, but spiritually strengthened and victorious, and how they stood up to the vices of discrimination, segregation, and agitation from evil people and systems. They were successful, because even though they could not see it, they believed it, and moved towards it without fear of what may happen in the process. My brother, when you truly believe in something or someone, you act on it. First you have to believe in yourself. Believe that whoever or whatever God has designed you to be is capable of doing and being what you've been assigned to do. Yes, you have haters and will always have them, but even they are there to keep you motivated; to encourage you to keep moving forward. If you weren't moving in your purpose, your haters would have no need to be hating because you would be miserable like them. When you rid yourself of the fear of failure, you open the door to immeasurable possibilities.

Remember my brother, royalty doesn't mean that you have to live in a palace or have tangible items that speak to wealth. You're of royalty because of the King to whom you belong. You're of his bloodline, and that will never change. You were created by God in his image and in his likeness–his royalty. Never let anyone make you feel that you are less than a personal design, crafted by the hand of God. You're a king and possess king qualities. The question is, do you believe you are of royalty and are you living your authentic kingship in your home, among your peers, and in your community? Are you the leader God chose you to be? Kings have rights and responsibilities. Kings do not surrender their kingship to the opinions of the people. Kings make sacrifices for the good of the kingdom and others. Kings are not afraid of a challenge and have self-confidence. Because they are of kingship heritage, they can conquer.

So, my brother, I say "rise up, O king, let your royalty be known. Establish your kingdom by your words and your deeds. Let your love as a king be made known to all. Fear not, O king, for what others may say or do, for your crown will never be taken unless you surrender it. Rise up, O king, take your place and set the pace for kings to come. You, O king, are of the Moses Factor!"

Dr. Norman L. Collins, Sr.

Dr. Norman L. Collins, Sr. is a father, grandfather, author, minister, motivational speaker, life coach and consultant who seeks to develop and promote holistic wellness and success and to help individuals recovering from various life challenges, tragedies and circumstances. His wide range of occupational experiences as a counselor, a pastor, an administrator, a mental health professional, and a consultant have enabled him to affect positive change in the lives of many. He is a proud member of Phi Beta Sigma Fraternity, Inc.

YOU CAN

Dear Brother,

I write this letter to encourage and challenge you. Whatever state that you find yourself in when you are reading this letter, I want you to know that **YOU CAN!** You can achieve whatever dreams and desires that you have for your life. You have been crafted by the great **"I AM"** and there is no doubt that you are one of his chosen vessels. The world is waiting on you, but you must be willing to change any negative behaviors and thoughts, listen, be humble, and be honest.

See my life's journey has been filled with many challenges and maybe you can relate to some of them. I am hopeful that you can use my story to gain the hope you need to move into your greatness. In 1971 at the age of 19 I found myself involved in a lifestyle and addiction that lead me in and out of prison over a 21-year span that included 17 years of being incarcerated. I did not care who I had to hurt in the process. And now when I look back on it, the only person I was hurting was myself. I was living a reckless life that often left me with lots of brokenness, anger, and bitterness.

Many individuals look at my life today and always ask, "What changed"? When this question is presented to me, I always say, "I got tired". One day I woke up to the life I was living, and I literally was TIRED! I was tired of hurting others while I was hurting myself.

I was tired of ripping and running in the streets. I was tired of being incarcerated. I was tired of being a disappointment to myself and my family. I was just TIRED! And lastly, but most importantly, I got tired of always having to watch my back. I realized at that moment, the life I was living and what I was doing to others was not right. After a 40-year span of low life living, in my tiredness, I found the energy to change.

To make my change, I had to change my thoughts and behaviors. I had to accept everything that I did and the consequences that came with them. I asked for help, went to treatment for addiction and behavior change. I surrounded myself with positive people that were going somewhere; individuals that held me accountable. I had to become honest and humble. I was steadfast in my desire to change and the results were great. Today I am a professional, a mentor for so many, and a testimony that YOU CAN!

If you are reading this letter and you are tired of the life you are living, you can make the change. However, you must realize you do not know everything. You must be willing to listen. You must shift your thinking. You must be willing to put the work in. The old saying, "hard head makes a soft behind" is extremely true. You must understand that you do not know everything. Be willing to allow individuals to teach and show you the way. This means that you will have to LISTEN! It is important that you listen to the wisdom from others. You will gain more knowledge by just listening versus talking. It is extremely important for you to shift your mindset. With my extensive criminal history, I always focused on "No one will ever give me a chance" or "I can't do that". I had to change my mindset to "I CAN" and "THEY WILL". Believing in myself allowed others to see my confidence. Most importantly, you must put the work in. Because I made the decisions in my life, I had to work extra hard to "clean my name" and show others that I was the changed man I proclaimed to be.

Remember that you are not less than because of your journey. We have all made mistakes and you should always hold yourself up high. The world is yours, but you must be willing to change.

Ollie Hooker

Ollie Hooker is a native of Raleigh, NC. He received his Bachelor of Science Degree in Psychology from Shaw University and his Master of Counseling Degree from Webster University. He is a Licensed Clinical Addiction Specialist with over 15 years of experience in the Health and Human services field. He enjoys mentoring and coaching others to fulfill their dreams. He is extremely active in his community and served on several committees.

BUILD WITH HUMILITY

Dear Brother,

It is amazing how when asked to be a part of this great feat, I thought about so many inspiring things I wanted to say. However, when it was time to start writing, it took me 30 minutes to figure out what I wanted my first words to be. As I was contemplating, I realized that my struggle to write this paper is equal to the struggle of life. One decision can make or break the arch of your journey. However, the beautiful thing about our journey of life, is that we are allowed to fall down, we build our character with how fast we get back up.

My personal favorite past time is coaching. I am one of the few coaches in my league, as well as all of the tournaments that we play in, that have our team join hands, make a circle in the middle of the court with all of our players, and publicly pray before every game. When we pray, we pray for both teams, not just our team. But the most powerful thing occurs after our prayer, and that is what we say on the count of three. The coaches ask on three what are we about, and the players respond: "HARD WORK AND DEDICATION!" Not only does this apply to the game of basketball, it also applies to life.

The toughest thing I had to learn on my journey of life was humility. This was instilled in me by my grandfather in my early adult years. I have been blessed to be in leadership roles for the majority of my career; however, when discussing work with my family, I always referred to my co-workers as my employees. I was telling my family, how a friend of mines from the neighborhood was now working for me. My grandfather did not correct me in a public forum, but a few weeks later he corrected me in private. He said Jamar, we all know you are a manager, so when you are talking about your job, we do not need you to continue saying someone works for you. They do not work for you they work with you–and you remember that. He went on to tell me that it can take you a lifetime to climb a mountain, but once you get to the top, if you slip, all of that work will be for nothing because you will fall. To help prevent yourself from falling, remain humble. And until this day, I do not say anyone works for me. So regardless of your status in life, remain humble. For from the dirt we are created and to the dirt we shall all return.

The Reverend Jesse Jackson said in 1984: *"I lived in old barrios, ghettos, and reservations and housing projects. I have a message for our youth. I challenge them to put hope in their brains and not dope in their veins. I told them that like Jesus, I, too, was born in the slum. But just because you're born in the slum does not mean the slum is born in you, and you can rise above it if your mind is made up. I told them in every slum there are two sides. When I see a broken window -- that's the slummy side. Train some youth to become a glazier -- that's the sunny side. When I see a missing brick -- that's the slummy side. Let that child in the union and become a brick mason and build -- that's the sunny side. When I see a missing door -- that's the slummy side. Train some youth to become a carpenter -- that's the sunny side. And when I see the vulgar words and hieroglyphics of destitution on the walls -- that's the slummy side. Train some youth to become a painter, an artist -- that's the sunny side. We leave this place looking for the sunny side because there's a brighter side somewhere. I just want young America to do me one favor. Exercise the right to dream. You must face reality -- that which is. But then dream of a reality that ought to be -- that must be. Live beyond the pain of reality with the dream of a bright tomorrow. Use hope and imagination as weapons of survival and progress".* So, I implore you to read the message above and apply it to your life, your struggle, or to your platform that you use to make a difference. If you feel that you are down and out, and at rock bottom, then there is nowhere to go but up. To make it to God's promise of the rainbow, you must first endure the storm. Therefore, whatever your skill may be, turn it into a weapon, your secret weapon, and use it to achieve the ultimate goal of true SUCCESS! Yesterday is the past, today is a PRESENT, and YOUR future is yet to be written, what will the next chapter of your life reveal? It is in your control to make it a memorable, POSITIVE one.

I would like to leave you with a quote from Dr. Martin Luther King Jr. I use this quote every time I give a speech to youth because it is the ultimate motivator. It states:

If you can't be a pine at the top of the hill, be a shrub in the valley. Be the best little shrub on the side of the hill. Be a bush if you can't be a tree. If you can't be a highway, just be a trail. If you can't be a sun, be a star. For it isn't by size that you win or fail. Be the best of whatever you are.

In High School I first wanted to be the best basketball player, but another brother had that title. I then wanted to be the best football player, but another brother had that title. I then set my sight on being the best public speaker, but another brother had that title. I spent the majority of my high school career trying to be the best at something. When really, I should have been attempting to be the best me. Do not set your sight on achieving a certain goal, set your sight and your goals at being a better person. Every day when you wake up, I challenge you to make "The Man in the Mirror" a better person. I say to you again, your past is done, your PRESENT is a gift, YOUR tomorrow, YOUR FUTURE, will be what you make it, make it a memorable tomorrow. How do you do that you ask? It is simple... You do it with HARD WORK and DEDICATION!

God Bless you!
Jamar Snow

Jamar Snow is a 2000 graduate of Crestwood High School and a 2005 graduate of the University of South Carolina. As he evolves in his life's goals, he continues to lift others up in their journey. He believes in keeping God first and always remembers the sky is the limit. He is a proud member of Omega Psi Phi Fraternity, Inc.

DECISIONS, DECISIONS, DECISIONS

Dear Brother,

From the time we are born until the day we die; we must accept the fact that we have the ability to make decisions. Those decisions may merit a reward, or they may cause us to suffer a consequence. This privilege is inherent to all humans. Men are taught we are to be the leaders, providers and protectors of our homes and communities. That principle is a lot easier to conceive when we are granted the benefit of not having to worry about how a bill will be paid or how food will be provided. However, when these benefits are not easily accessible, having to live up to those expectations can be difficult, which unfortunately has caused some to make decisions that are not favorable in the eyes of the law, leading to the incarceration of some. It is during these times, that some reflect upon their actions and re-live the "what if" moments of life.

If only I had done it differently,
if only I thought before acting,
if only my life situation was better,
if only my father was present,
if only I made better grades,
if only my mother loved me more,
if only my siblings did not pick on me,

if only I was not bullied in school,
if only I had not been molested,
if only I were not given everything I wanted,
then my life would have a different result.

It is true that we are all products of our environment, but we don't all have to be victims of it.

When we look at men who have come from various backgrounds, it must be acknowledged that what might be expected may not occur. For instance, boys who grow up in financially, comfortable families have ended up on the street. On the other hand, there are others who have grown up in socio-economically deficient environments that have gone on to become financially successful. The results of the men, in these two vastly different backgrounds, were not based on where they were physically. No, it was about where they chose to be mentally. We are who we believe ourselves to be. It doesn't matter what your parents, your teachers or your associates say. What matters is what you say about you. Just because a path has been laid before you does not mean you have to follow it, especially when you see it leads to destruction.

If when we find ourselves in situations that are not the most positive, we cannot blame outside elements. We must also stop blaming ourselves, and instead admit responsibility. There is a vast difference. We walk where we have chosen to place our footsteps. The winds of adversity did not blow us into whatever our current situation is, it was how we chose to weather the storm. When we make choices, we must be bold enough to stand on those choices. If we did it, we did it. There will be some that will forgive us and some that will not. But the most important factor, is that we forgive ourselves. This process is not always easy, nor is it impossible, it simply takes time and a willingness to want to move forward in positivity.

A slogan, a saying, and for some, a mantra "if it is to be it's up to me" has been said to many. However, no truer words have been spoken. At the point in our lives when we have our "a-ha" moment, when the light bulb comes on, when we realize we should have had a V-8, those words should be paramount in our thoughts. Whatever is going to take place for the betterment of ourselves, our community, or our world, begins with what we do to make it better.

Wherever we are, we have the power to change our environments for the better. We have not just a responsibility, but we have the privilege of being able to use our experiences to encourage, to inspire and to motivate those around us, and around the world. We may never know the impact of what we share about where we have been or what we have been through could possibly prevent someone from making some of the same decisions we have, or prompt someone to make the same decisions depending on the outcomes, negatively or positively.

For far too long we have been led to believe that we live our lives for ourselves. To a degree that is true. But the greater truth is, we live our lives for each other. We all possess something that someone else needs but will never receive if we do not allow that which has been placed in us to come to the forefront. A student of mine, when she graduated, gave me a shadow box with the inscription "somebody somewhere is looking for just what you have to offer". Michael Jackson penned the words "I'm starting with the man in the mirror". When we as men allow that change to occur within us, then we can bring that change to the world around us. In order for that to happen we must understand who we are, not compared to those around us, but compared to our individual self. We must take inventory of who we were, who we are, who we have yet to become, and use those as a basis of self-evaluation. As we grow up, we should be working on growing out. We should be adding to our circle and expanding our horizons, absorbing all we can so that when the time comes, we will have something to share with those we encounter.

Today is the day, now is the time. As you read these words, let this be the moment you start doing those things your future self will be proud of. Whatever has been done, even up until now, has been done. We cannot "un-hear" what we have heard, we cannot "un-see" what we have seen, nor can we "undo" what we have done. We can however use those occurrences and experiences for growth and development. The knowledge gained from the tragedies we survived yesterday, are for someone else to be able to triumph tomorrow. We survived the abuse, the breakdown, the depression, the infirmity, the eviction, the loss, and the success, to show someone else how to handle it and not be consumed. There are times life will knock us down, but as long as it does not knock us out, we are still in the fight. Sometimes we feel like what we have endured has left us half-dead, but the joy is that half of us is still alive. It is that part that lives in all of us that gets us up when we want to stay down, that moves us forward when the winds of opposition want to push us back.

Our greatest gifts have yet to be unleashed. Just like the purest of gold, or the most valuable of precious stones, their true value is not immediately revealed. Like gold that has been put in the fire, or like a diamond that has been cut and polished, these unpleasant processes were necessary to determine and eventually present them in their best forms. Like those natural stones, if we want to be pure, we must first be purged. We must let go of all the scrap metal that diminishes our value. If we want to be the highest quality of diamond, we must surround ourselves with other diamonds, for only a diamond can cut a diamond. This is not to say that we are better than anyone, because none of us is any better than the rest of us. What it means is that when we realize what is really in us, we will be more willing to endure the necessary processes to bring it to the surface. We must realize that until we learn to let go of the trivial and understand if we, as men, begin to lift and empower each other, we can then lift and empower worlds. But this all hinges on what we shared at the beginning of this... we must accept the fact that we have the ability to make decisions, all of which will merit a reward or cause us to suffer a consequence. We carry a great weight, we carry a great responsibility, but when we carry them as we have been designed, then and only then can we unleash the power that comes therewith.

Dr. Dwyane N. Elam

Dr. Dwyane N. Elam is a native of Petersburg, VA. and raised in Chesapeake, VA. Upon graduation he attended Norfolk State University where he studied Business Administration. When discovering the finite borders of that curriculum did not allow room for his creativity to flow, he entered Hicks Academy of Beauty Culture. When he graduated he received his diploma and certification from the Clairol company as a colorist. In 1995, Bro. Elam graduated from the National Institute of Cosmetology with a Ph.D. in educational sciences. For over 25 years, he has been a cosmetic art instructor, where he has the opportunity to share information and knowledge that has transformed the lives of many. In 2008 he answered the call to ministry and is a licensed as a Local Deacon at Emmanuel AME Church. He is the Husband of Mrs. Angela E. Elam. They are the parents of three adult children Mario, Adrian, Kristina and the grandparents of four, Cayden, Brady, Sosa, and Solei.

A LETTER OF LOVE AND LOSS

Dear Brother,

Hmm, a little about myself... My pen name is Joseph Wrights, but I go by J. Wrights, which the name itself is also a long story. I am 44 years old and a single father of three: a son, 19, from my first marriage, and two daughters, 15, and 12, from my most recent. I was in the military for 8 years and then joined Homeland security. I joined a few companies afterwards, building my technical experience. I also went back to school to achieve my Bachelor of Science in Business Systems Administration and Information Technology. I now work as a Deputy Program manager for a Fortune 500 company called Jacobs.

I am by no means rich, but I have led a pretty interesting life. Although I am pretty comfortable now, I acknowledge my struggles that have allowed me to personally define success, which I could not have done without meeting the most important person in my life, Abby. Meeting her was chemistry, like harmony twisted on its side and spread to infinity; to the place where we touched. Losing her was the hardest moment of my life. But from the very beginning, she taught me so much, she was my muse, and she inspired me by showing me that life has no limits. No rules if you will. And gave me a taste of what you can achieve by not holding yourself back by simply saying, YES!!! If only I could have told her how much she impacted my life, if only I could have said thank you one more time, if only...

I met her in Brooklyn, New York, when I was 18. It was so unexpected, and quiet that night on the streets of the city. It was a beautifully clear evening and me and my girlfriend were going to meet up with one of my best friends, Sharon, as well as her family to go to a house party. We were walking across the street to their apartment building, which just so happens to be on the first floor, when a girl was looking out of one of Sharon's windows. It must have been a full moon that night, because I could see her face so clearly, especially her eyes. It felt like we had met before, because when she turned and looked my way, our eyes met. I felt something I had never felt before in my entire life, a connection, unlike love of a parent or love for a sibling. I could not explain it, but I had known this woman my entire life. I thought to myself, "Who is that?" Well, I thought I was saying it to myself, but no, my girlfriend heard me, and she said, "WHAT!" I tried to explain it away, like guilty people do, but she was no fool, and she watched me like a hawk the entire night. But I didn't care, because as soon as I entered the house, and Sharon introduced HER to me as her cousin, nothing could stop providence!

"This is Abby," Sharon said.

All I heard in my mind was, "This is the woman I will be spending the rest of my life with!" She was young, and it just so happened to be her birthday. She had the aura of a more mature woman, she was stoic, but I could tell she wanted to meet me. Maybe she heard me from outside that window, but I didn't know. What I do know is that when we came face-to-face, she laughed as she shook my hand. The memory of our first meeting is ever fresh in my mind.

So we go to the party and the night went well, except for one part- my girlfriend didn't like the instant connection Abby and I made. Eventually, she said she wasn't feeling well and left early that night.

I tried my best to be attentive to her, but I was mystically distracted by a presence I couldn't predict or understand. I offered to leave with her, but she declined saying she wanted me to have my fun. Again, I didn't understand, but I didn't turn down the offer either (Dumb and Young). I walked her to the cab, and she left. I stayed downstairs a bit to get some air while I tried to figure out how I was going to explain this to her tomorrow, but I was soon interrupted. Sharon came to check on me, but she wasn't alone, Abby was with her.

Sharon asked, "Is everything okay?"

I said "Yes, but I think we might be breaking up."

Abby chimed in, "Was it my fault?"

What a loaded question, I thought to myself, because I felt she knew it was. We were looking at each other all night without a care for my girlfriend's opinion on the matter.

I said, "Noooo, we have been in danger of separating for a while, but we will see tomorrow". She then asked, if I was leaving, and I said no, and she said, "If you want to talk about it, we can." Sharon gave me a look and instinctively went back upstairs to the party.

We talked outside until it was time to go, everyone came outside, and I saw Sharon and her sister. They had called a cab to come pick them up, the rest of us lived nearby. I walked Abby, along with her cousin, and mother, home. Yeah, the whole family was there. As I reached their place they asked if I was hungry.

I said, "YES!"

They invited me upstairs, we ate, and then Abby put on music. She and her cousin started dancing to Soca. It was late, but this is how Guyanese people enjoy music, and I loved it. Her cousin was tired, and he went and sat down, and eventually nodded off. I just watched as Abby gyrated to the Caribbean rhythms, and I was in heaven just being in her presence. She must have read my mind, because she asked me over, and I never felt more nervous in my life. As I approached her, I felt as if there was electricity between us. The closer I got to her, the stronger the intensity of my feelings became. We danced slowly, then as if on cue, I looked down at her, she smelled so good, and as I thought this, she looked up at me, and smiled. She came closer and I felt as if a new universe was created as our lips touched. It was a sweet touch and reminded me of mangos. We were entwined for what seemed like an eternity, but closer to a few minutes. It's funny, I use to always say "I Love you more," whenever she said to me, "I Love you!" As I write this I now, I realize that as much as I loved her, she loved me even more, and that love was joy personified and realized in our love for each other.

You would think this was the beginning of a beautiful story, and it was. It's just unfortunate that my story has so many ups and downs, and nerve-wrecking plot twists. Too many to write here. Maybe one day I'll get the courage to write more.

Sadly, after 23 years of love, laughter, tears, reunions, and sadness, it came to such a sudden, yet peaceful end. Where the love of my life, my soulmate, my queen Amirah. Or rather Cherish, a name she later became known as, would pass away just after her 38th birthday. It was almost to the day when I met her, just a few weeks, and a little over two decades where we had our first kiss and LOVE came into our world. It was a Sunday... a sad day.

I remember that before I met Cherish, I was aware that my life had a higher purpose. And I thought I had truly found it, until I met her. She introduced me to something more, as she told me a few days before she departed this physical plane, "This was not the end!" But instead, her end was truly the beginning of my own life, a rebirth perhaps. I began applying everything we learned together to my own life and became a new man. I have learned that it is so important to respect and love every moment of your life, because every second is a precious gift from the lord. Like I mentioned before, these were her words as she said goodbye, "Everyone is in your life for a season and a reason. I've given you mine and I know you'll be greater than you can ever imagine, if you just let it happen!" It's an amazing feeling when someone believes in you more than you do yourself. And I couldn't believe, as she laid in the bed of a hospice, that she was consoling me, preparing me. I could not have loved this woman any more than I did right at that moment. It was like the first day I saw her, in that window on East 95th and Kings Highway, my heart was hers all over again, and I held her close and told her how I felt. A tear came from her eyes, as tears also fell from my own. I thought in this moment… I was truly blessed to know this woman. Blessed indeed!

I would like to speak on all that I have learned, but there's too many lessons to speak on here. So, I'll talk about the most important takeaways from this major loss to my heart and soul as best I can. It's difficult to put into words, because even as I grasp the understanding of what I learned, it's more like they've become things I should have always known. I mean, what's the point in being with someone, creating a life with someone, if not to share the roles and responsibilities of the life you now share.

Losing my partner meant I had to learn about myself all over again; sounds strange right? Well, I had to first admit that I'm not as whole as I thought I was. Whether that meant being a whole man, or a whole person, that's irrelevant. What matters is there was an emotional "incompleteness" to my center, which were due to my auto-dependencies to Cherish.

The first sign of this weakness was being able to express my emotions, as a parent versus as a man when it came to my children. This relearning wasn't as bad with my son as it was with daughters, but that emotional support I had to provide was definitely needed for him as well. I was a patient man already, but I had to couple that with listening and understanding on levels I never knew I had to, in order to provide what my children needed. I'm not saying I became this perfect parent, not at all, but I had to become less closed fist and more open hand in my handling of specific situations.

Another lesson, for which I blame entirely on society's sexual ste-
reotypes, especially those on responsibility and ownership in the co-
parenting household. We, as men, take for granted many of the
things women do for family. I had to not only manage the house
more, and the kids, but I had to speak more on an emotional level
with my ailing wife. And do, well, everything. Like learning to do
my little girls' hair and teaching them feminine things like makeup. I
even tried to teach them how to knit, but the most uncomfortable
subject to this day is talking about boys, especially because I know
them so well. Luckily my young ladies are older now, so they tend to
piggyback off of each other more, but I still have to be readily available and vigilant when it comes to the subject, because I can't just
say "NO", or "good luck" to the subject. I have to remain objective
and supportive, while providing neutrally, yet subjectively, sound
advice. This includes my son as well.

I truly feel that these types of subjects shouldn't automatically be
labeled male or female and put in the box where only girls learn and
teach girl subjects, and likewise for boys. For example, If I say the
word "housework", I bet you automatically thought woman's work,
right? How unfair. My saving grace is that I came from a matriarchal
household, and my mother spent a lot of time with us. In spite of that
upbringing, I still reached out to many of the women in my family
for sound advice and fellowship.

Which leads to my last lesson to discuss, which is, that you cannot do this alone! Without the love and support of my family,
Cherish's family, our friends, our neighbors, my family therapist,
coworkers, and especially my church's Reverend at that time. I don't
know if I would have gotten through this very emotional period in
my life, intact and in my right mind. These folks held me together
more than they would ever know. Whenever I was in pain someone
knew somehow and reached out to me. Whenever I needed support,
they made time without question and without judgement! Whenever
I needed a break, because I had to sometimes just stop because it was

too much, they allowed me to take a deep breath and take care of myself; they held out a helping hand and gave me the time I so desperately needed. That old saying, "That it takes a village..." is absolutely true! Being a single parent, shouldn't be as literal as some people make it out to be. If it is that literal to them, then they should definitely rethink their approach to parenting because it's a lot of pressure for one person, especially when you're still grieving as I was.

Finally, I also want to especially thank God for supporting me! He got me through a tough decade, and still carries me even now. As I watched my wife fight and struggle for another day of life, it encouraged me to be grateful and humble for every second of life I have and for every sunset I am blessed to witness. I just hope my short lesson on humility and discovery of one's self doesn't bring sadness to whoever reads this, but instead brings hope and encouragement, that we as humans can survive and overcome any obstacle in our very short life through perseverance, the revelation, and acceptance of our own weaknesses. For this is how we become better in life and can one day achieve greatness, if we allow it!

Jeremiah 29:11 *""For I know the plans I have for you," declares the Lord. "Plans to prosper you and not to harm you, plans to give you hope and a future.""*

Job 11:18 *"And thou shalt be secure, because there is hope; yea, thou shalt dig about thee, and thou shalt take thy rest in safety."*

Joseph Wrights

Melvin Wactor is a native New Yorker by way of Brooklyn and goes by the pen name Joseph Wrights. He is 44 years old and is a widowed single father of three - His son, 19, and two daughters, 16, and 12. J. Wrights served in the Army for 8 years, and then joined the Department of Homeland security for 3 years before moving to Baltimore, Maryland. He has a degree in Business System Administration, and a minor in Information Technology, and is currently a Program Manager with Jacobs. He is an aspiring chef, writer, poet, and also performs Life Coach and Mentoring work to those who ask for it.

THE VALUE OF BROKEN PIECES

"There is no better than adversity. Every defeat, every heartbreak, every loss, contains its own seed, its own lesson on how to improve your performance next time."
— Malcolm X

Dear Brother,

Let me start by simply saying, **"You Are Enough"**. Life will sometimes make you think and feel that you aren't enough because you come from a different place and your struggle and story is different from the rest–do not believe the lie. If you are not careful, life will trip you up, having you to believe that your worth is minute and minuscule. There is a magic power that is locked inside of your being and it is waiting for you to unlock and unleash it–it's called PURPOSE. You have been placed in our world to make a change in our lives.

Throughout the process of life, you will experience some broken pieces. You will have to deal with broken family issues, broken friendships, broken relationships, broken dreams, broken hopes and even a broken spirit. And in some cases, you will not have caused the brokenness, but you will be forced to deal with it. But I encourage you to hang on to those broken pieces. Never allow a broken situation to make you feel as if you've lost because you have not. Use it as a learning tool. It will be those experiences that will help mold you into the KING that you are destined to be. Through faith and determination, you will one day be able to create a beautiful masterpiece out of all of those broken pieces. So, in the meantime, learn all that you can from those broken pieces.

Never forget to forgive. Sometimes issues and circumstances will arise in your life, which will cause you to either have to apologize or to accept an apology. Never be so stubborn that you do not know how to forgive or to be forgiven. Alexander Pope once wrote, "...To err is human, to forgive divine. All people commit sins and make mistakes. God forgives them, and people are acting in a godlike (divine) way when they forgive." You are human, and you will make mistakes; and vice versa–the people that will come in and out of your life are human as well and they are prone to make mistakes as well. However, always be willing to forgive. Forgiveness gives you freedom. Sometimes you have to: **#1** – Forgive when no apology is offered, **#2** – Delete their number and text thread (remove them from all social media outlets), and **#3** – LIVE and LOVE your life. Learn to take a breath between each step and simply move on. You have so much to give that you cannot waste time dealing with unforgiveness.

I am the man that I am today because of the wisdom imparted in me by my late grandfather–David. He was the greatest grandfather, but most of all, an amazing example of a loving man. I grew up in a single parent home with a strong, fierce and loving mother who did the very best she could with molding her three sons into Kings. However, there were times when I hated life because I did not have the "picture perfect" family; furthermore, for the fact that there were times when we had to struggle. It took me many years, many tears, and many letdowns to really understand this thing called life. I hated my father because he was not there to teach me how to be a man; neither was he there to protect me as he should have. While I had many role models and mentors, I still wanted my father. Yet, he chose drugs over his son. I had to realize and accept the harsh reality that I could no longer allow my dysfunctional childhood to be a legitimate excuse for my bad decisions in life. I simply had to GROW UP. I had to learn how to forgive and move forward.

My grandfather David once dropped some life changing knowledge on me that I want to hand down to you. He simply said, "Don't let your life run you, instead, you run your life." In short, you have to man-up and take control of your life. Do not allow your circumstances, past situations, failures and dysfunctions, to control your life, but you must stand tall and take that control back and change the outcome. Life and death are in the power of your tongue. Take charge of your life by speaking positivity, truth and the word over your life. Learn how to use the power of your words and the power of prayer in order to align your life with the will of God. I promise, he will make the path clear.

Do not allow life to dictate your happiness, your peace, your sanity, nor your joy. Take authority of your life by trusting God's plan for you and make no apologies for protecting who you are. I am the first to admit that sometimes trusting God can be hard when you have so much coming up against you at once, but you must continue to stand on the word of God. Let the power of your memory push you. Remember all the other times where you felt hopeless and faithless, and then remember what God brought you through. How he made a way and came through for you. He had your back and desires the best for you. Be sure that you expect the same for yourself.

Word to the wise: be careful of those who you confide in and who you call your friend. You must be selective of who you entertain in this season of your life. Our lives transpire in seasons. Seasons are connected to people. So, if something is wrong in your season, check who you are connected to. Sometimes you need to simply send a message of RELEASE or PAUSE! Some of the people in your life you need to RELEASE and let GO. They are not helping you in any way–they are simply distractions. They love mess, they start mess, they thrive in mess, they keep mess going-LET THEM GO! You'll thank me later. Some people you have to put on PAUSE! Not everyone in your life is bad, it may just not be their season to be an active participant in your life. Their presence in your life right now could throw you off course. And if they really mean you any good, they will understand that this time of separation is for you to get yourself together, so you can LIVE YOUR BEST LIFE!

Word to the wise: be careful of having so many faces in your face. Some people are sent into your life on assignment to keep you from unlocking your destiny and unleashing your purpose. Some will come looking good, smelling good, and talking a really good game, but YOU BETTER WATCH! Talk is CHEAP. These faces can take both physical and spiritual forms. Be selective of who you offer VIP status in your life. Everybody does not need the red-carpet treatment, and everybody is not worthy to have that kind of access to you. Be mindful of the spirits that you entertain. You should always strive for "Good Vibes Only". If someone's spirit does not click and something is off–RUN! That can block what God would like to do for you and in your life. So, it is best for you to be careful of what faces you allow to be in your face.

I want you to know that I am so proud of you. I am proud of the man that you are becoming; the man that the world is going to love. If you fall, get back up. If you feel that you need to cry–cry! Know that crying does not make you weak, but it is those tears that will water that seed of greatness that is within you. If you fail–regroup. Failure means you have a blueprint of success for the next time! If you get tired, take a break–self-care is vital. If you get frustrated, chill out–it's a part of the process. If you need answers, seek God! I promise you that he will never steer you wrong. If you ever need encouragement, simply look around–you have so many brothers that are rooting, supporting and lifting you up. You will succeed because defeat is not an option. Be who you are, and the world will LOVE and RESPECT you.

Above all–know that I love you and I am rooting for you.

Love & Light,
Rev. Justin M. Barbour - "Your Brother"

Reverend Justin M. Barbour - an Author, an Award-Winning Scholar, and an Influential Educator is a proud graduate of Fayetteville State University where he obtained a B.A. degree in English Literature and Language. In addition, he is a graduate of Concordia University – Portland where he obtained a Master of Education in Educational Leadership. He serves the Senior Pastor of the Smithville A.M.E Zion Church of Cheraw, SC. He is currently an adjunct professor at Central Piedmont Community College and is a Board Member of Power Moves Education & Consulting. Above all - he humbly serves with a spirit of excellence and efficiency.

WISDOM FOR THE JOURNEY

Dear Brothers,

As you journey through life, please utilize these quotes to inspire you, encourage you, and motivate you.

"Everything is a process. They key is what you do in the process. It will determine the outcome of how fast the process will be."

"Leadership is not defined by a title. Leadership is defined by what you do with the title."

"Through obstacles, comes success."

"You want to be sure you are moving in the right direction and striving to make progress. And if you look back to where you came from, and you're not continuing to gain knowledge or progress, then one has not grown in life."

"Life is like art; you paint the picture of how you want your life to be."

"Our life's mission, while on earth, should not just be to accomplish our goals and desires. We must extend a helping hand when needed, to help others achieve their goals and dreams."

Brothers, if you apply these words to your life, you can accomplish your dreams. You must believe in yourself and always be willing to serve mankind. I charge you to share these words with others. The world is waiting on you.

Sincerely,
Carlton Rowe

Carlton Rowe is a native of Raleigh, NC. He holds a Bachelor of Business Administration from Strayer University. He is active in his community and has served as a mentor, advisor, and in leadership to various organizations. Carlton has been appointed to a variety of different committees and boards, most recently Mechanics & Farmers Advisory Board. Carlton's number one goal is to provide economic opportunity by enhancing economic mobility to drive financial success for the current and future generations.

SURVIVORS

To all of my Misunderstood Brothers,

As I sit in my room and I think about the life of a black man in America, I just don't understand why we are always misunderstood. But there is one thing that I do know-we are SURVIVORS.

They say we aren't anything and we will never be anything, but I beg to differ. Some 400 years ago we were Kings and Queens. We owned land, cattle and had strong family values. We were taken from our home and brought to a strange land, separated from our families, publicly humiliated and some of us were killed. But we had God, and we SURVIVED.

Then they say we were free as long as we remained in our lane. Walk on that side of the street, go in the back door to eat. And no matter how long you been on your feet, get up and stand when the white man needs a seat. They killed our little girls at 16th street Baptist Church, and demoralized our son-RIP Brother Till. Still, my hat goes off to Rosa Park for taking a seat, Dr. King for taking a stand, and for all my strong brothers and sisters who crossed that Edmund Pettus Bridge. Once again, they had God and they, SURVIVED.

It eventually got a little better, but they tried a new trick. We didn't own any boats, planes, or trains, but for some strange reason drugs over ran our streets. It was such an overwhelming blow, and we didn't know where to turn. We watched our brothers begin to rob, steal, and kill. We cried when we saw our sisters sell themselves, lose their kids, and live on the street. Then we woke up and got back on the right track thanks to the cornerstone of each and every one of our communities-the Church. Some were Baptist, some AME, some just store front, but they continued to do for us what we didn't really know we needed and prayed. They kept us with God, and we SURVIVED.

We prayed and prayed, and God then answered. We got that education, we got those jobs, we can go where we want and eat what we want. It got so good until we even saw our dear brother, Barack Obama, become the 44th President of the United States. Just when we thought we were over the hump, one more time they tried to stunt. They put on uniforms and pulled us over. Now the ones that are here to serve and protect us have started to harm and disrespect us. But still my brothers, don't live in fear because we have God and we're going to SURVIVE.

Well my brothers, I now see why we are so misunderstood. Time and time again we get dealt a bad hand and a great deal of the world cannot fathom that no matter how many times we are given some lemons, we will make us some good old lemonade. You see, we understand that there is always somebody talking about us, but really, we don't mind. They are trying to stop and block our progress. Most of the time, all of the mean things, that others say, can't make us feel bad because we can't miss a friend we never had. But we have God, and that's enough. When we're sick, He's there. In times of trouble, He's there. Being oppressed, He's there. When we are misunderstood, He's still there. And He always answers our prayers. So, to all of my black brothers, and yea I'm talking to you Pookie, Ray-Ray, Chugg, and Whispers-keep your head up. It may seem like the world is against you at times, but if God is for us, who can be against us. So, stand tall and be the black man that you were created to be and understand that all of your dreams are still in your reach. Just remember to keep your hand in the master's and I promise you if you keep God, you will SURVIVE!!!

Peace,
Mark Wood

Mark A. Wood II, is a native of Grasonville, MD. He accepted his calling to preach at Robinson AME Church and was licensed as an Exhorter. As a man of God, Exhorter Wood is always diligently working within and very faithful to the body of Christ. He has been and remains an encouragement of the youth, especially the young men. Every day that passes his mission is to try and make a difference in the world by reaching one soul at a time. In 2015, Exhorter Wood married his lovely wife, Raychelle, and together they are the proud parents of four children Mariana, Mark III, Markayla, and Markel. He is currently employed with RDU International Airport. His mission is to try and make a difference in the world by reaching one soul at a time.

HOW TO GET THERE

To My Young African American Brother,

I am Marcus Shields. I was born and raised in South Carolina. I was educated in the schools that many refer to as the "Corridor of Shame." I did not let the labeling of the public schools, that I attended, hinder me from excelling. I went on to graduate from high school with honors and attended the University of South Carolina, at Columbia. At a predominately white institution of higher education, I soon learned that I was just a number. I went on to graduate from undergrad in three years with honors. Having a strong desire to be of service to others, I went on to law school at North Carolina Central University School of Law and obtained my law degree. It was there that I learned that I had to strive to be greater than good. After law school, I entered into the practice of law, determined and committed to never forget where I came from, while maintaining an intent to help every soul I encountered. Today, I preside over courtrooms as a judge in the great State of North Carolina.

To my young, African American brothers with dreams and ambitions I say to you: "You can." All things worth having are not easy to obtain. Never let anyone tell you what you are capable of. Surround yourself with people who affirm you and motivate you to be better. Never settle for second best. Aim to set the bar high for not only yourself, but for those who you bring up from behind you. No matter how high you ascend, never forget where you started. Never forget the people who carried you and cared for you from day one. Humility is a gift you should always be willing to receive. The key to achieving is believing in yourself. Never start a sentence with "um." Be confident when you speak and know that you are always good enough for a seat at the table.

"Getting there" may not come quickly and without obstacles. Keep up the momentum. My young, African American Brother, know that sometimes moving in silence is key. Never let everyone know what your next move will be. Achieving goals, manifesting dreams and ambitions require you to plan accordingly and adjust when necessary. When you achieve your goals, reach back and encourage the next brother to be greater!

In Truth & Service,

Hon. Marcus A. Shields

Hon. Marcus Shields is a North Carolina District Court Judge for Guilford County. He is a graduate of the University of South Carolina and NC Central University School of Law. Prior to becoming a judge, Marcus Shields practiced as a private practitioner; a post-conviction attorney for NC Prisoner Legal Services and as an Assistant Public Defender for Guilford County.

FEARLESS IN PURSUIT OF
TRUTH AND LOVE

Dear Brother, What I want you to know….

Since the establishment of modern civilization, there have been tireless efforts created by people of European descent to classify, demonize, and systematically erase who you are and what contributions your people have added to this world. From the time of the European "enlightenment", every person of color throughout the world, has been defined as a savage. An onslaught of imagery and definition(s) have been purposeful in demonizing who you are, and what you represent! The question you have to ask is "Do the images and definitions that I see, from any media source, really represent me and what I stand for?" Dr. William Cosby and Dr. Alvin Poussaint were proficient at showing positive, black representations. Every show they produced and aired was scrutinized carefully to determine if people of African descent were represented in a positive light, on a national platform. Why is it necessary to be represented in a positive light? There have been countless studies that confirm media imagery affects a person's perception of self. The question is, what are you watching and who do you believe you are as a result?

What I want you to know is that things you read in this book are TRUTHS that will not be aired on TV, viewed on many "SNAPS", or posted on the "GRAM."

What I want you to know is that you have constant thoughts that give you a clue to what your purpose is on this earth. Your ingenuity and intelligence, in the most basic things, give credence to what your people have operated with for eons. I want you to know that anger and frustrations are to be controlled by first finding the root cause to your problems with one another. You need to identify ways to express your feelings through words and expectations. I want you to know that being in any relationship requires you to establish boundaries. The boundaries* you set for others; ensure you feel safe at all times. I want you to know that walking away from toxic people* is ok. I want you to know being around strife, fighting, arguments, or constant disagreements IS NOT NORMAL! If you can identify that your girlfriend or boyfriend are not respecting you, or your boundaries, the relationship will never work. Media has shown us reality housewives, that bicker and fight constantly. This is not normal behavior, nor will it ever be. Constant arguments or strife within any relationship does not equate to someone loving you. I want you to know that walking away from adverse situations makes you a better person. Before you react to any situation, take time to think. Ask yourself this question: "What does this mean in the grand scheme of my life?" Questions like this make you think about the good and bad consequences of every decision you will ever make.

You are a part of a fearless generation. The problem is that this "superpower", causes you to make ill-informed decisions that produce negative consequences. Being fearless is a great tool, if used for the betterment of yourself or others. I want you to know that your norm does not have to be your reality. Some of you reading this are saying: "I can't wait to get out of here!" Here being, school, parent's house, job, etc. But what are you going to do when you get out? What is your plan? How will your plan be successful? In this life, success should only be measured by the positive impact you have on others. Consider this example. When most HBCUs were created, many people of color were sent to school with the bare essentials. Between the college itself and boarding houses* situated around the school, the student had their basic needs met, all while obtaining an education. When those students graduated and began their careers, who then was credited with their success? The answer is ALL–it took a village. The village played a role in that student's success! No one is better than the other. Someone has to sacrifice for you to succeed, like you need to sacrifice for another to succeed. Our current society does not believe in or adhere to this model of humanity.

I want you to know that priorities and morals, in our society, have become so tainted that the reality of what is truly important is blurred. Political correctness, being considerate, and words like inoffensive and inclusive are all real terms that have theoretical premise. However, they have been replaced by people having basic empathy towards one another. It has become a common occurrence to hear merciless comments from government authority and religious leaders. This unapologetic stance has continued to permeate how we treat one another. The truth is, every person is our inherent brother and neighbor. We are commanded to love one another. If we believe every being is our brother or sister, we are then tasked with keeping them. If we have an allegiance to mankind, then we have a duty to celebrate their successes and be compassionate towards the short comings of our fellow brothers and sisters.

Love, keeping an allegiance towards someone, requires empathy. I teach an empathy intelligence tool within my group therapy sessions. The tool requires one to be introspective and extrospective simultaneously. During any adverse situation, you should ask yourself, "What do I feel?" and "What do I need?" Then ask yourself, "How might they feel?" and "What might they need?" This exercise helps you to determine what you need to make an empathetic decision by considering your brother's/sister's feelings. What is of most importance, is that you realize the responsibility you have towards each other. Lastly, what I want you to know is that the Lord is God. It is important you believe in a higher power. I personally have been saved by the blood of Jesus! I fully recognize that some may feel like this is the "white man's religion". But I ask that you CONSIDER the source by which your people were introduced to Jesus. Our people were forced to believe in the Lord from the guise of control, in order to keep us "tamed", and produce profit for the slave master. Jesus came to set captives free. This is an oxymoron! The believer comes to know The Lord through confession and an experience. I admonish you, if you have not already, ask Him for a personal experience to know Him and I guarantee He will show Himself and guide your steps accordingly. I love you all with the Love of Jesus, it is truly the highest power and love that I know.

Michael Adams

Michael Adams is a native of Bridgeport, CT who currently lives in Garner, NC. He is a human service professional who currently works within a batterer's intervention program. By educating, training, and teaching clients to succeed in forming and maintaining healthy relationships, he believes that healthy relationships can become the cornerstone to live a peace-filled lifestyle. Michael is happily married to his wife of 15 years and they have two children together. Michael has several certifications in the field of human services including: PREPARE/ENRICH, ACES trainings, and intervention strategies for addressing family trauma. Michael is a soon-to-be elder in his local church and holds a B.A. in Psychology from Saint Augustine's University, M.A. in human services from Liberty University, and is a doctoral candidate in human services cognate in criminal justice and trauma at Walden University.

COMMAND YOUR COMPANY, CONDUCT, & CONVERSATION

Dear Brother,

Throughout my lifetime I must say that I have indeed encountered many words of wisdom and encouragement; however, quite often my mind goes back to the fall of 2013. I was a freshman at Morris College in Sumter, SC. I will never forget Mrs. Sherry Harvin; she was my professor for freshman seminar. Every time we met for class, she would have us repeat the prayer of protection–you may or may not know it, but it goes like this:

The light of God surrounds me,
The love of God enfolds me,
The power of God protects,
The presence of God watches over me,
Wherever I am God is,
God is everywhere

One of the things I admired about Ms. Harvin is that she always spoke life into us and always shared words of wisdom with us. One day she said to us, "Young people, in college and in life, you must be aware of the 3 C's." She went on further to say, "You must be mindful of your company, conduct, and conversations." And if there are any words of advice that I can share with you, it's the words I received from Ms. Sherry Harvin: be mindful of your company, conduct, and conversations. I believe if we all follow Ms. Harvin's words of advice, there is no way that we can go wrong.

Company. In middle school, every morning our principal would get on the intercom and make a few announcements. Once he was done, he would close by saying, "Show me your friends and I'll show you your future." What he was intentionally saying was that I can tell how far you're going to get in life based on who you hang around. He was also saying that whether you know it or not, but if you hang around somebody long enough, you'll begin to do the very things that they do.

In High School, I hung around people who skipped class, so I began skipping class. I hung around people who had tattoos, so I began getting tattoos. I hung around people who drank, so as time passed, I found myself drinking. Whether for good or bad, who we hang around can impact us tremendously. It's amazing how we as young people can go out of our way, trying to be like somebody else. But as you read this, I dare you to do yourself a favor. Don't try to fit in with the crowd, because if you're constantly fitting in with others, how can you stand out?

You have to constantly ask yourself the question, are the people I'm associating myself with really who I should be hanging around? In other words, are they helping you or are they hindering you? Walking away from the wrong crowd is never easy, because you fear being talked about and you fear being alone. But know this one thing, elevation, requires separation. The place God has for you, everyone can't go there with you. If you've ever been on an elevator, you'll notice that everyone who gets on with you doesn't always get off with you, and when people exit your life, sometimes you've got to rejoice because some people you're connected to will cause you to miss the very thing that God has in store for you.

Whatever you do, don't lower your standards to please so-called friends. One of the hardest things I've had to learn, is that some people don't love you for you, but rather love you for what they can get out of you. Many people will tag along because you have a car and aren't charging a dime for gas. Many people will tag along because you're always spotting and paying for them. Stop allowing people to treat you like a backup plan. They only hit you up when they feel like it or in need of something. Make up in your mind that you're not putting up with individuals who take out of you more than they invest in you.

Conduct. Before you do anything, think about those who love you-will your decisions bring shame and dishonor, or will they bring happiness and joy? It is often stated that perception is reality. With that being said, how you dress determines how people treat you. I like to tell all young men that no one will take you seriously if your pants are hanging off of your behind. Pull up your pants and begin to dress for success. Young women your clothes don't have to be so short and you don't have to be so loud just to be seen. Someone will come along and love you not for your body but for who you are as an individual.

Conversations. Mamma and daddy would oftentimes say if you don't have anything nice to say, don't say anything at all. Believe it or not, sometimes it's not what you say, it's how you say it. I'm reminded of a story. There once was a little boy who had a bad temper. His father gave him a bag of nails and told him that every time he lost his temper, he must hammer a nail into the back of the fence. The first day the boy had driven 7 nails into the fence. Over the next few weeks, as he learned to control his anger, the number of nails hammered daily gradually dwindled down. This young boy discovered it was easier to hold his temper than to drive those nails into the fence. Finally, the day came when this boy didn't lose his temper at all. He told his father about it and the father suggested that the boy now pull out one nail for each day that he was able to hold his temper. These days passed, and the young boy was finally able to tell his father that all the nails were gone. The father took his son by the hand and led him to the fence.

He said, "You have done well, my son, but look at the holes in the fence. The fence will never be the same. When you say things in anger, they leave a scar just like this one."

The reality is, words can sometimes hurt more than when you are putting your hands on someone. But the very truth of the matter is, no matter how many times you say I'm sorry, the wound will still be there.

As you go throughout life, just remember the 3 C's, your company, conduct, and conversations. God Bless.

Rev. Jake Sanders III

Rev. Jake Sanders III is a native of Sumter, SC. He is a 2018 Magna Cum Laude graduate of Morris College, where he graduated with a Bachelor of Arts degree in Christian Education. Rev. Sanders currently resides in Atlanta, Georgia where he is pursuing his Master of Divinity Degree (MDiv.) with a concentration in Psychology of Religion and Pastoral Care at the Morehouse School of Religion. He is the Pastor of Calvary Baptist Church in Chester, SC. Rev. Sanders' two favorite scriptures are Psalm 34: 1 "I will bless the Lord at all times and his praise shall continually be in my mouth" and Luke 6:40 "A disciple is not above his teacher but everyone who is perfectly trained will be like his teacher". Rev. Sanders is a proud member of Alpha Phi Alpha Fraternity, Inc. Catchall Masonic Lodge No. 425 (prince hall affiliated) and Catchall chapter No. 315 OES. Rev. Sanders also serves his community, state, and country while being enlisted in the Army National Guard. His Motto is: In a world where you can be anything, be nothing but yourself.

DESIGNED FOR A PURPOSE

Dear My New Brother & Friend,

I was born to a single-mother and did not know what life would reveal to me. The first woman to capture my heart, other than my mother, was my grandma; we called her Mu. She and my grandfather introduced me to Jesus Christ. I was always in church singing and working. I was exposed to individuals who were blue collar workers. They were plant[factory] workers, office cleaners, and fast food employees. These were the only careers that I knew of as a child. As my life continued, I grew, and I questioned the episodes of my youth. Why were we (my mother, my siblings, and I) forced to move from house to house? Where is my daddy? Why don't I have the things my friends have? Why does my mama keep saying she doesn't have money? Why are we moving in with my grandparents? Why don't we have running water in the house? Why did my grandparents have to die? Why can't I ever fit in? Does my family really love me? You may have some of the same questions and experiences I had as a young black man, but understand, there are answers to your questions and purpose in your experiences.

Despite those things that your life may expose you to, I offer the following advice. Stick with God and work your faith! Life will always throw curveballs at you and the devil will be right there in your ear with a negative message trying to convince you into making the wrong decisions. Always stand your ground because you know who you serve and where your help comes from. Just remember all the times God has made a way and brought you out before. Always remember, if HE did it back then, HE can and will do it again. This is what you call faith! Remember, you are never going to fit in, even though you have always tried to do this. Why are you wasting your time? Stop it! You were designed to be different; you were designed to be the trendsetter; you were designed to make a difference by being uniquely you... DO IT! In your younger years, you may have seen your people work as plant workers, office cleaners, and fast-food employees, and you knew they wanted better for you. You can attend any Ivy League college or university and achieve your dreams. My friend, you are well on your way! Keep pressing because there is more for you to accomplish.

My friend, when it comes to your family, be mindful of two concepts: love and death. Although you may not always understand them, remember when confronted by either you have the ability to both pray and cry. Society says men do not cry, but that is a lie! Crying is a symbol of release. And remember, always pray. This is directly related to your connection with God. This is a connection that should always be open!

With these words, I encourage you to continue and be great in your own right! I am proud of you no matter what! I love you!

Blessings,

Michael D. Finkley

Michael D. Finkley, GCDF, M.Ed., M.S.Ed.

Michael D. Finkley is a native of Mullins, SC where the teachings of his mother and grandparents stemmed his spiritual background. He is a graduate of Allen University (2011) and a two-time graduate of Southern New Hampshire University (2015 & 2018). Finkley is the Founder/Executive Director of The Finkley Experience, LLC where he assists his clients/students in the following clusters: College Readiness, Career Readiness, Tutoring, Empowerment, and Professional Training. He wants everyone to know the sky is NOT the limit, aim towards the moon! He is a proud member of Alpha Phi Alpha Fraternity, Inc.

ALWAYS BELIEVE IN YOU

Dear Brother,

I want to start this letter by first congratulating you on believing in yourself. I want you to know that you can accomplish what your heart desires. Just remember that with anything you put your mind to, always stay committed. You can achieve your goals. Never doubt your mental toughness, it will ensure your commitment to accomplishing your hopes and dreams.

You are a leader, and one of your qualities of being a leader is having the mindset to never give up or give in due to your circumstances. Although things may not always be easy or line up the way we want, never stop believing in yourself. Frustrations may sometimes creep into your mind, but I want to encourage you by saying don't allow those moments to cause you to overlook the opportunities that are available to you. Surround yourself with others who will encourage you along the way. We all need people in our corners who will be an encouragement to us. We also sometimes need these same people to remind us that we are somebody.

Life is full of transitions, which sometimes means we need to transition people out of our lives who aren't speaking "life" into our situations. As the Bible tells us in Proverbs 18:21, "Death and life are in the power of the tongue." So, there are times when we must evaluate those in our inner circle who may be trying to keep us stagnant, in other words, feeling like we can't go any further. It's important to surround yourself with others who will encourage and push you along the way. Those who push you to "keep on keeping on".

I hope this letter will encourage you, as we all need encouragement to always bet on ourselves. Always believe in yourself. Even when you are presented with obstacles, stay the course. Know that you are intelligent. You are a smart individual who will not allow circumstances or situations to stand in your way. I'll end by telling you this. When people doubt you or question your abilities, remember as the Bible tells us in Matthew 19:26, "With men this is impossible; but with God all things are possible". So, when others doubt you, remember it's possible!

Simeon Hutchinson

Simeon Hutchinson is a native of Savannah, Georgia and a graduate of Shaw University where he received his Bachelor of Arts degree in Mass Communications. He also has a Master of Education degree from Liberty University with a specialty in School Counseling. He is currently employed as a School Counselor with Wake County Public School System. He accepted his call to ministry on November 4, 2012 and was licensed to minister the Gospel in March 2013 in the African Methodist Episcopal Church. Since then he has been on the move for Christ through preaching, teaching, mentoring the youth and other activities. He is married to the love of his life, Reverend Terri Hutchinson. Together they have three beautiful daughters.

CHOICES

Dear Brother,

Not all, but many of us were raised by a single mom without a father figure in the home. This could be for any number of reasons: incarcerated, deceased, a dead beat or simply, the relationship didn't work out. Despite any of that, she [your mom] did the very best she could to raise you. She most likely had struggles of her own, which ultimately contributed to where you are in life right now. You probably had brothers and sisters in the home as well. In many cases, single mothers have a hard time receiving child support. Surviving without the financial support from the father places a significant strain on a single mother who is not already established. Without a decent income or support system, it is almost impossible to afford decent childcare or after-school programs where you could be cared for while she is away, working. To compensate, she will most likely end up moving the family somewhere she can afford, which is usually in a low-income neighborhood. She may still have had to work all kinds of odd hours, leaving you home to fend for yourself, just so she could keep food in your belly. But never enough money for the latest Jordans, and yet she would still find a way to get them for you. This showering of gifts likely was a byproduct of guilt. Guilt for not having your father in the home. This unwarranted guilt also leads to her not pushing you very hard; fearing she may push you away. Some of us, wanting to be a man and help our moms will try and figure out a way to bring income into the home. This is where the problem may begin. Choices. Life is about choices. You can use life's hard times against your family as an excuse to make money any way you can, including stealing or selling dope. It's easy, it's quick, and it ain't really hurting anyone... until it does. You may cross this line thinking, "I'll only do it for a little while" or "They are going to buy it anyway, why not from me?" This type of thinking is not thinking at all. A little while usually never comes. People begin to see you as that "guy". Cops start seeing you as that "guy". Your mom starts to see you as that "guy". And more than not, you'll start smoking it yourself. It becomes your job. Years pass. You are 26, still living at home with mom, playing video games, smoking and selling weed. Of course, this is a best-case scenario. Rewind. Choices. You can use life's hard times in your favor. Decide that your family will have better. Get a part time job at McDonald's to help your mom. Lock down your schoolwork. Graduate. Get a degree. Get an awesome job. Move. Then people will start to see you as that "Guy". Your brothers and sisters will look up to you knowing that if you can do it, they can do it. Your mom will say, "that's my son, I am so proud of him," as tears stream down her cheek. Even the other kids in the neighborhood will see you as a role model. This choice is easier than you think... Proverbs 3, verses 5-6 says, "Trust in the Lord with all thine heart; and lean not unto thine own understanding. In all thy ways acknowledge Him, and He shall direct thy paths." Life is all about the choices you make, and the choices are yours to make.

Troy Hill

Troy L. Hill is a native of South-Central Los Angeles. He was raised by a single mom with two brothers and two sisters. He grew up in the 70's and 80's when gang violence was at its peak. He found Christ at an early age and has been covered with His grace ever since. Troy served in the US Marine Corps for 8-years. He is married to the love his life Nichette Hill.

YOUR CHALLENGES ARE BUILDING YOU

Greetings Brother,

Adversity truly introduces a man unto himself. No matter where you are in your life, you will always encounter challenges. These challenges are not placed to deter you from walking your path toward greatness. No, they offer the opportunity for you to build character during your journey. Inspiration creates dedication and dedication inspires creation. Failure is not an option, because failure is not assured. When we struggle, we learn lessons. And from these lessons, we learn success. Falling down multiple times and getting up defines resilience. Everyone has fallen before, but everyone doesn't get up. Living in and serving low-income, and disenfranchised communities, helped me to understand how challenges and imperfections shape the people we become. I envision a world where young black professionals can create businesses and opportunities for generational wealth in low-income and disenfranchised communities. Generational wealth presents a gap, one that we must all come together and strive to close. In order for Blacks to be liberated we must first unite, educate and love one another. We always talk about how 1 dollar only lasts 6 hours in the black community, but we never discuss how long it takes 1 dollar to enter the black community. To my black men and women, in all urban and rural communities, to you I say this. We must establish equity and transparency in wealth by developing an infrastructure that helps create sustainable revenue.

Additionally, we must reinvest that revenue back into our communities. We have always been oppressed, stereotyped, and marginalized. This coincides with a lack of educational/professional development, equity, mass-incarceration, and low socio-economic status. In order to change our communities, we must alter our minds. We must move towards becoming a part of the decision-making bodies for our communities. We must strive to revise policies and procedures that marginalize black communities. We have to build coalitions, movements, and institutions that provide political education, encourage faith-based religious practices, build pantries that minimize food and clothing insecurities, establish support in mental and physical health, create programs that allow families to receive cost-effective child care, [improve] Medicare, and educational support. These adversities may seem like obstacles but remember that God gave each and every one of us the same tools to be successful. These challenges are not placed to deter you from walking your path toward greatness. Again, they offer the opportunity for you to build character during your journey. Be dedicated and inspired, because inspiration creates dedication, and dedication, inspires creation.

Brandon S. Douglas

Brandon Steven Douglas is currently employed with Wake County Human Services as a Human Service Senior Practitioner. He is a 2009 Graduate of East Mecklenburg. He earned his Bachelor of Social Work and Master of Social Work from North Carolina Central University. He is a member of the Raleigh Alumni Chapter of Kappa Alpha Psi and serves as the Keeper of Exchequer, and Vice Chairman of the social action committee.

WHAT IS YOUR
PERSONAL STATEMENT?

Dear Brother,

"Life's battles don't always go to the stronger or faster man. But soon or late the man who wins is the man who thinks he can." These words, written by poet Walter D. Wintle, express the importance of having faith in one's personal ability to accomplish goals and reach new heights. It can be argued that faith is the starting point of all achievement. During times when there is a lack of motivation, faith in your ability to be disciplined will enable you to take the next step. During times when things do not go as planned, faith that things will turn around enables you to see it through until the end. In short, faith is that little voice in your head that says, "You can do it. Most importantly, you are WORTH it."

Oftentimes, African American males lack a sense of personal faith. This can usually be traced to the negative portrayal of African American males in the media, or the systematic oppression that plagues our communities. How can one have faith in their abilities when society constantly tells or treats them as if they do not matter and will never amount to anything other than an athlete, rapper, or drug dealer? Well I can assure you that this is not true. As a young

African American male, I had to come to the realization that I had to believe in myself. If the world is already against me, I could not also be against me. We must be our biggest advocates. Although this is not always easy, it is necessary. There are countless opportunities and they are all waiting on the right person. Why can't that person be you? Regardless of your upbringing, educational level, or economic status, you have something to offer. You have a talent that no one else possesses. And it is your responsibility to present it to the world.

Under no circumstances am I an expert, but I am someone who had to regain faith in myself. I searched everywhere for an answer. I turned to the internet and YouTube for motivational videos. I read books and turned to family and friends. Nothing seemed to work and like many others, I almost gave up. Eventually I came across the book *Think and Grow Rich,* written by Napoleon Hill. In this book, I discovered the principle of auto-suggestion, or rather, positive affirmation. Essentially, it is the idea that one can develop personal faith and achieve goals by "tricking" themselves into thinking they can. As humans we have the ability to control our thoughts and actions. Our actions are influenced by our subconscious mind, which is influenced by our experiences and what we choose to believe. Oftentimes we internalize things that we see in the media or have been taught to believe as true. Consequently, our perception of the African American male is not always positive. Through my experience, I have summarized what I believe to be the three key components associated with making the practice of auto-suggestion beneficial to shifting one's state of mind. Although they will not lead you to instant success, they can help get you on the path to success if effectively practiced.

The first component is defining the goal that you wish to achieve. The goal must be definite in regard to what you desire to achieve, the time frame in which you want to achieve it, and what you are willing to give and/or sacrifice to achieve it. This is perhaps the most important component, because it forces you to look inward to decide what you truly want in life. It is also an opportunity for you to define your own version of "success". Think about what matters to you. Think about your purpose and how your actions can benefit you and those you care about.

The second component is developing a personal statement that outlines your goal and how you wish to achieve it. This statement is critical, because essentially you are creating a contract with yourself. It does not have to be long or complicated either. It can simply be what your goal is, the time frame, and the ways you plan on achieving your goal. An example of one of mine is, *"I, Wayne Russ II, DESIRE to accumulate $1,000,000 by December 9, 2026. To achieve this DESIRE, I will reduce the urge to spend excessively and frivolously, dedicate free time to learn and develop lucrative skills, and not seek to impress others through material possessions. I will earn the $1,000,000 through the income streams from my career, investing and day trading, and real estate."*

The third component is daily repetition. Each day I write and recite this statement three times, twice a day, once when I wake up and again before going to bed. I write and recite it when I wake up to remind myself of my goal before starting my day. By doing this, I am intentional about carrying myself throughout the day in a way that moves me closer to achieving my goal. I write and recite it before going to bed with the hope that I will be able to internalize it by dreaming about it. It is critical that you do this every day without pause. The more you do this, the faster you can internalize it and begin to act in ways that reflect your desire.

Furthermore, I would like to clarify that by simply doing this you will not achieve your goals. This is just the starting point in shifting your mindset. Achieving goals requires a success-oriented mindset in addition to application. In other words, you cannot expect to achieve goals by just saying you will achieve them. This has worked and still is working for me, so it is my hope that it will work for you. Remember: you are your biggest ally and supporter. There will be people who will support you along the way, but it starts with you. I believe in you and you should too. You can do it. You are WORTH it!

Wayne Russ II

Wayne Russ II is a native of Sumter, SC. He was the 2015 Valedictorian for Crestwood High School. He holds a Bachelor of Science degree in Finance and Accounting from the University of South Carolina. In his professional career as a Corporate Client Banking Analyst, Wayne has proven himself to be an invaluable asset in many capacities. He has served as the Vice President of Professionalism for the National Association of Black Accountants. He is a proud member of Alpha Phi Alpha Fraternity, Inc.

CHANGE YOUR LOCATION

Dear Brother,

First, I would like to say, anything is possible with the right mindset and dedication. If you already know what you want to do in life, find the individuals that are currently in that position and let them be your guide. Watch their career actions, as well as the results of those actions. If the actions yield great results, then consider molding those actions into your lifestyle. Conversely, if they achieve results, you just saved yourself time by now knowing what not to do. If you know the individual personally, that's great! You can ask questions. But if you don't know the individual, just observing can be good enough. Don't limit this to one individual. For example, I'm a Landscape and Portrait photographer, so I watch other photographers in the same field that I deem successful. I observe to learn what they are doing that's possibly furthering their career; actions that I can possibly mold or add to my own.

The elements mentioned above are meant to help guide you and possibly save you some time, but not necessarily copy exactly. Other elements, like your attitude, location, and planning for the future, ahead of time, will also be beneficial to you. You will need a great attitude to connect with people to build a network that will serve you this year or 10 to 20 years later. The person you meet today can be the same person that determines whether you get the job or close on a deal. Don't be afraid to change location if what you're seeking isn't available in your current location. A change of location can be a difference of not being able to land a position or not being capable of affording a desirable home. Consider scouting multiple locations for the best outcome for you. Your future is always closer than you think. Prepare accordingly. Educate yourself about retirement, so that you will be able to maintain a certain lifestyle when you're no longer working. Know how long it takes to become a vested partner at your job or know where your money is being invested if you're self-employed.

Keith Jackson

Keith A. Jackson is a native of Sumter, SC. He has worked in the medical profession for over 15-years. He is also a professional photographer that utilizes photography as a method to promote self-love and boost self-esteem among his customers.

IT'S YOUR TURN

Start where you are, with what you have.
Make something of it and never be satisfied.

-George Washington Carver

This collection of writings was designed to empower and motivate you. We love you as our brothers. View this body of writing as a toolkit, how might you proceed on your personal journey. Below you will find reflection questions that will aid your initial steps in drafting your own letter; for pure reflection, for encouraging another, or to simply tell your own story. Just as we took up this responsibility in designing this book, we now hold you accountable to continue. **It's your turn.**

1. What are some words of wisdom that you desired to hear from your father, grandfather, uncle, etc., as a child?

2. What might you say to a young African American Male that has dreams and ambitions, but is unclear of how to get there?

3. What might you say to a young African American Male that is currently incarcerated and is ready to throw in the towel?

4. What might you say to an older African American Male that is facing a challenging illness and/or dying?

5. What might you say to an African American Male that is struggling? Being Bullied? Lacks self-esteem? Does not fit in? Feels devalued?

6. What might you say to your son (born or unborn)?

7. What might you say to yourself?

Dear Brother:

_____

_____

_____

_____

_____

_____

_____

_____

_____

_____

_____

_____

_____

_____

_____

_____

_____

Your Brother,

Meet the Visionary

Jason T. Mahoney
www.jtmahoney.com

"Crafted to educate the mind, enhance self-awareness, promote inner strength, and motivate change"

Jason T. Mahoney was born to stir up the gift in everyone he encounters, and it is for this reason he is "**The MOTIVATOR**". His gifts as a speaker, emcee, author, poet, and stage performer have motivated individuals to harvest the seed that has been planted in them.

He is a bold man who is captivating and possesses a powerful presence that will challenge you, inspire you, and mold you.

A native of Sumter, S.C., Jason was always taught the value of love, discipline, and hard work. He has worked in the health and human services field for more than 15 years. He currently holds a Bachelor of Science Degree in Sociology and a Master of Science Degree in Counseling. He is credentialed as a Certified Family-Centered Trauma Coach, Qualified Mental Health Professional, Life Coach (Individual & Family), and Certified Family Wellness Instructor.

Throughout Jason's career he has been a featured keynote, workshop presenter, emcee, coach, consultant and trainer. He has been featured in *The Artise Magazine* for his work as an author and community philanthropist. He was also a guest on the *The Positivity Push* 103.5 WCOM FM Radio Show.

Jason is the accomplished author of *Four Faces of a Revolution*, *Tried in The Fire*, and *Edification on The Go*. His ultimate goal is to educate the mind, enhance self-awareness, promote inner strength, and motivate change. It is his motivating approach that has individuals feeling empowered to take back control of their lives.

CPSIA information can be obtained
at www.ICGtesting.com
Printed in the USA
LVHW050716081019
633524LV00011B/932/P